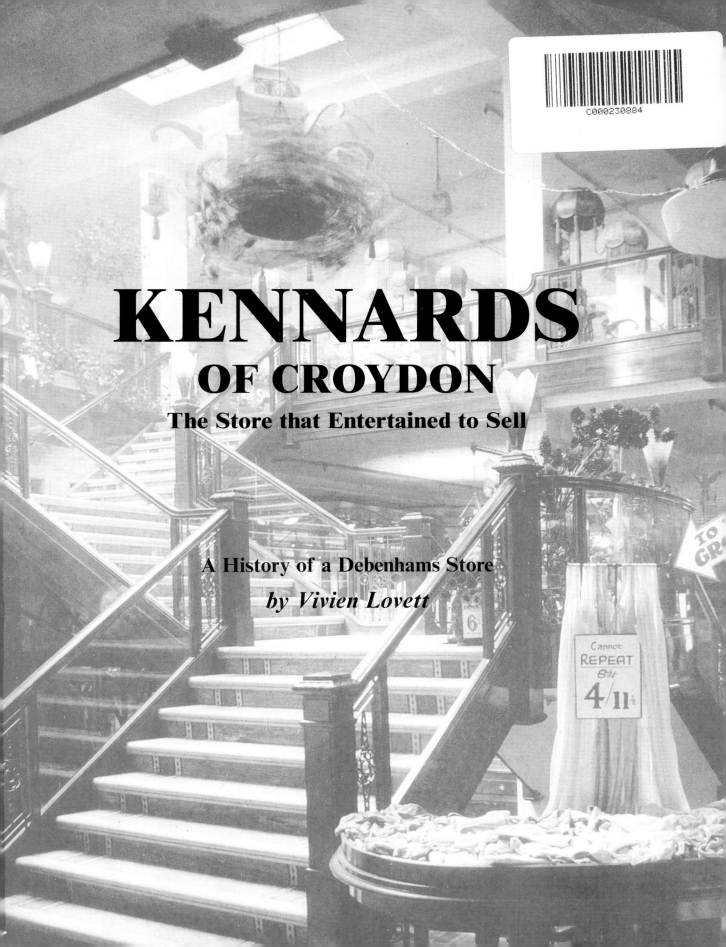

KENNARDS
OF CROYDON
The Store that Entertained to Sell

A History of a Debenhams Store

by Vivien Lovett

KENNARDS OF CROYDON
is dedicated to my dearest husband Leslie Whitehouse,
whose continued support and encouragement enabled me to write about this unique store.

Front cover
top left: North End *c.* early 1900s
top right: Kennards North End *c.* mid 1930s
bottom left: White elephant sale *c.* mid 1930s
bottom middle: Ida Santerelli and her girls *c.* mid 1930s
bottom right: Kennards sales counter *c.* mid 1930s

Inside cover
Main staircase *c.* late 1920s

Back cover
North End *c.* 1890s

Epilogue
Pen and ink sketch - 'forget-me-not' by Vivien Lovett

ISBN 0-9537968-0-9
First published 2000 © Vivien Lovett

Published by:
Vivien Whitehouse
No. 2 'Larkhill', 51 Great Woodcote Park,
West Purley, Surrey, CR8 3QT

Edited by:
Derek Bradford

Printed by:
Litho Techniques (Kenley) Ltd.,
46-50 Godstone Road,
Whyteleafe, Surrey CR3 0EA

CONTENTS

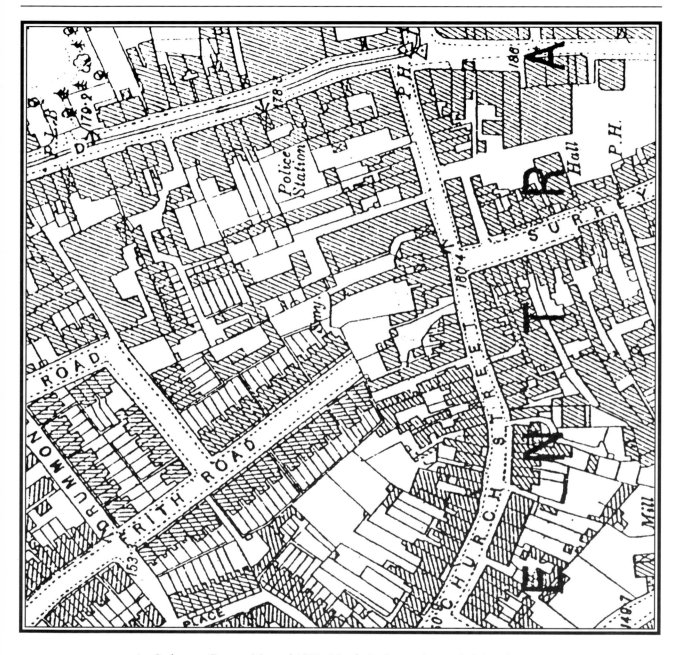

An Ordnance Survey Map of 1895. North End is in the top left hand corner.

FOREWORD

I was delighted when Vivien Lovett asked me to pen a few words as a foreword to her latest book. I, together with most people whom I meet from the South East, particularly of my generation, have vivid memories of riding on a pony down Kennards' arcade. Undoubtedly this was the highlight of a child's visit to the store in the 1930s. My earliest recollection is of a ride on a model steam train on the roof of Kennards. Later I remember lunch in the restaurant with my brother Colin, when we had to be on our best behaviour under the stern eyes of our grandmother "Mrs. William", who was regarded with equal awe by all members of staff and possibly even her husband! I was in fact the last member of the family involved with the store and my connection ended shortly after the name change in the 1970s.

Vivien has carried out an enormous amount of work in her research for this publication and I would heartily recommend it as a most interesting account of the growth and development of the great store. The pre-war slogan "Where goods cost less than they should" epitomised the policy in those far off days. I wish the book every success.

William Robin Kennard
(Great grandson of the founder, William Kennard)

INTRODUCTION

What made Kennards of Croydon, "The Wonder Store of the South", so popular a place where people came, not only to shop, but to be entertained too? Kennards' original ideas made headline news on a national and international scale.

The public saw famous invited guests such as film stars, sportsmen and national figures. The department store claimed to be the first of the larger stores in the environs of London to introduce a Christmas Toy Fair, an arcade of shops and Shetland pony rides. It also boasted to be one of the first to launch a National Savings Drive and an exchange of vegetables for clothes during World War Two, together with a Grower's Vegetable Market.

Throughout its heyday Kennards maintained a multitude of interesting and unusual attractions to entice the whole family to this delightful department store for the entire day. The relationship between management, staff and customers reveals the social attitudes of the period.

The story of the growth of the store from its humble Victorian beginnings makes fascinating reading. By 1935 the store occupied a ten-acre site, employed over 1.200 staff and served eight million customers a year. The store not only served 'Croydonians' but also customers from all over the Southern Counties and was very appropriately termed "A Town within a Store".

The chapters that follow are concentrated on Kennards from its Victorian inception to its change of name to Debenhams in 1973 and subsequent demolition in the early 1980s. The story of the existing 'modern' Debenhams is left to future historians.

This book will reveal a department store that was ahead of its time. Kennards was unique. There was probably never a store such as this before, nor ever will be again.

Little Acorns

William Kennard, the Founder of Kennards, c. 1880s

Mr. William Kennard could never have guessed that, from a tiny acorn sown, a great oak in the form of a department store, renowned for its unusual departments and attractions, would have grown and survived for 120 years. Kennards store grew to a size unprecedented south of the Thames. The seed rooted well and blossomed into what was to become Croydon's most popular and enterprising store, drawing customers from miles around.

Mr. Kennard's original double fronted shop, which was a Linen Draper, Silk Mercer, Shawlman and Furrier was situated in North End, Croydon, where its most recent successor, Debenhams, now stands, but was previously occupied by a hair-dresser, pewterer and ironmonger. Records reveal that Kennards was established by 1853. As was the custom in those days most tradesmen lived over their shops, as did Mr. Kennard, although by 1864 he was residing in a private residence, No. 1 Cavendish Villas, Wellesley Road, Croydon. William Kennard, with only one assistant to help him, would have spent long arduous days at his shop starting at 6 am and finishing at 9 pm with opening hours that extended to 11 pm on market days. The daily 'takings' had to be counted, account books kept, parcels wrapped and delivered, stocks checked and displayed and more stock purchased. In those days it was considered a large shop. The 'dressing' of the store would have looked rather peculiar to us today as most of the stock hung from the ceiling, space being very restricted. There would have been two sales each year with winter and summer being the 'highlights'. "Attractions" or in-between sales were not really an event in those days.

Early records show that in its first year of open-ing this small store, which measured 60 square metres, was set up by the founder with a capital of a little over £100 served 8.000 customers. It was Mr. Kennard's policy of selling reliable goods for cash, at very low rates of profit, that soon enlightened him that this particular policy was the best one to adopt in the interest of the public and business alike. It was not long before he realised that he needed to obtain further premises if he was going to meet the needs of his ever-increasing number of customers. More detail comes from a John Heath, founder of a firm of sign-writers, who ran a toy and printing shop in North End. He enlightens us that Mr. Kennard, who had just started out his business, startled his fellow traders by adopting the revolu-tionary idea of having window tickets on his goods, seemingly unheard of in the provinces. Fixed price ticketing was established in the London stores as early as 1830. It was usual to haggle or bargain with the shopkeeper as one would with a hawker or street trader in those times.

William Kennard's double fronted shop could have remained a good old established business, where personal service was of prime importance, but Croydon was rapidly expanding from its small market town status. Several major factors brought about the development of Kennards' shop and other drapery shops into department stores. Originally the industrial wealth in England, proudly viewed at the Great Exhibition of 1851, created a new 'middle-class' spending population. Great importance was attached to the outward signs of prosperity such as handsome household furnishings and expensive clothes. The 'family' and its requirements became of prime concern to the trader. Another main factor was the improved railway service, which brought shoppers into the larger towns. This rapid change encouraged the growth of family businesses such as Kennards and its Croydon competitors, Joshua Allder and Grant Bros. The heart, the very hub of life in Croydon at that time centred about the High Street, North End, Church Street and the 'triangle', of which Surrey Street remains, so William Kennard's shop was well situated.

William Kennard outside his shop in North End c. 1870s

Branching Out

North End, looking North.
The old Police Station, Kennards' shop and Buckworth Drapers can be seen on the left, c. 1890s.

In 1886 William Kennard brought in one of his sons, 'Mr William' to help with the business and the shop fascia became Kennard (W) & Son. Shortly after, William Kennard was on his own again as the "new blood" and the old did not mix well. By the following year, in 1887, William Kennard had died. 'Mr William' joined forces with his brother 'Mr Arthur' and in 1890 they renamed the shop 'Kennard Bros'.

View of 'Kennard Bros' in North End, 1893.

The Kennard family shop 'Warwick House' Nos. 7 & 8 North End was "devoted to the sale of linens", trading in a small way, but within a short period of time the family began to expand their business. (North End's street numbering was changed in 1886 and Nos. 7 & 8 became 15 & 17). In 1892 Kennards also occupied a shop opposite, No. 16 called 'Manchester House', but business ceased in this shop in 1896. In this same year Nos. 11 & 13 North End (the site of the old Police station) was added and in 1907 Kennards' lateral spread extended to 23 North End. The premises of Messrs Buckworth, who had also been family drapers, at Nos. 25 to 31 North End became available and these were added to Kennards' collection in 1911 and all done without borrowing a penny.

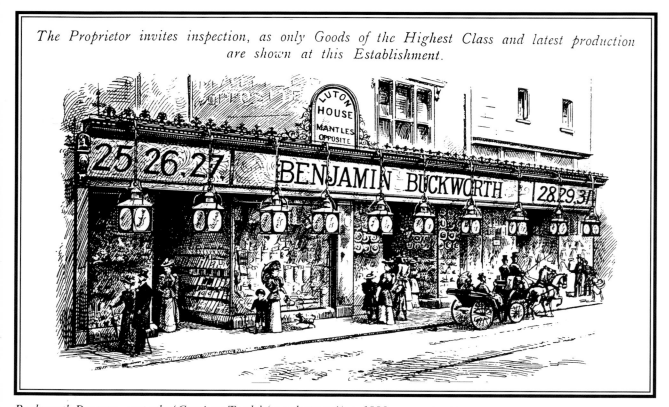

The Proprietor invites inspection, as only Goods of the Highest Class and latest production are shown at this Establishment.

Buckworth Drapers – note the 'Carriage Trade' (see chapter 4), c. 1890s.   *Reproduced by kind permission of the Croydon Advertiser Group*

By 1911 the entire block of premises was rebuilt, giving the whole building a harmonious look. A system of arcades or walkways with full-length island windows ran the entire frontage of the building. (This will be referred to as the North End arcade to avoid confusion with the Frith Road and main covered arcade, which were not yet built.) The North End arcade enabled the shopper to study Kennards' merchandise at close quarters without inconveniencing the passing street pedestrians. Inside these windows saleable goods such as furs, robes, blouses, mantles (coats), under-linen, rugs, floor cloths even, were displayed.

Kennards expansion 1911.

Above: A portion of an interior arcade in 1909.

Left: North End arcade. This arcade was one of the largest in the country and contained over ¾ mile of windows, c. late 1920s.

Kennards devoted its stock "to which ladies were interested", for, in those days, most customers were women. Once inside the store, from Nos. 11 to 31 North End inclusive, every department could be visited without going out into the street.

The packaging and despatch rooms opened out onto Hedgis Yard. Customers' purchases were despatched twice daily by motor van. Deliveries were originally by hand cart and by 1906 Kennards had 11 horse drawn vans. Shortly after they hired a single cylinder 8 hp. De Dion-Bouton motor van and bought the famous 'Napier' vans. These were in service until the early 1930s.

Kennards' delivery fleet, c. 1920s.

Above: Kennards' delivery fleet c. mid-1930s.
Right: 'Men At Work', but time to pose for the photographer, c. early 1920s.

There were no further extensions to Kennards during the dark days of the 1914-1918 war. In 1920 a small block was added to the rear of the store, together with a new main entrance in North End. It was still a two-floor concern (basement and ground floor) apart from a frontage strip, some 25ft deep, which had three floors. A year later Kennards made an upward move and the whole store became a three-floor establishment, there being no further opportunity to expand sideways.

In 1923 another three floors were added to the rear block and in 1926 Kennards branched out once again. An additional four-floor building was erected and completed in May 1928.

This new building was on the site of Riley's Billiard Hall at the rear of Kennards. It doubled the floor space so badly needed making an area of no less than eight acres. In spite of all this increase in showroom space the frontage and window space remained the same. Department after department

had been added but only half of them could occupy the window space at one time. More windows were needed, but extension sideways was not possible. The solution was to move all the ground floor departments further back with the rearmost overflowing into the Billiard hall building, thus leaving space on the North End frontage for yet another new window display in keeping with the rest of the store. This display took on the form of a magnificent arcade 50ft deep, which stretched the whole length of the North End front. In the centre of the arcade was an entrance hall leading to the new main entrance, which was over 50ft wide. This was a period of major development in Kennards' history and a very ambitious and successful scheme for its time making the premises quite unique amongst larger stores.

Top: The erection of the first floor showroom extension which opened in March 1923, c. early 1920s.
Bottom: Kennards' North End frontage 1923.

An interior window display in the North End arcade, c. late 1930s.

Only the North End arcade existed when the 'in store guide' of the late 1920s stated: "If Kennards' famous window arcades were straightened into one long sheet of plate glass, it would reach from George Street, Croydon to Croydon General Hospital. The floor space of the arcades alone accommodates 2.400 people; this floor space is tiled with 1.617.800 ceramic tiles which, if placed end to end, would extend for over 20 miles, or if placed on one another, would form a pillar 6.67 miles high!"

Grants', Allders' and Kennards' growth like that of the town itself, had increased rapidly as public demand had grown. Kennards recognised that if it was to maintain its high standards it not only had to be abreast of the times but ahead of them. By mid 1930s it was catering for the weekly wage earner section of the community. Working class women became more clothes-conscious, more home conscious. Kennards' policy had constantly been to draw in the public with something different. It added more attractions to its "shopping centre" and many an advertisement read "A Town within a Store" and was aptly named because it housed a vast range of goods and services.

Top left: A showcase arranged for a Window Dressing Competition in the North End arcade, c. late 1930s.

Bottom left: The main entrance in North End in 1923.

The Man Behind the Store

In 1921 'Mr William' Kennard felt the need of another pair of hands to assist him so he made cautious enquiries for someone whom he could trust to help carry on the business. Did such a person exist? He most certainly did!

He was born in 1884 and came from a town 'up country' in New South Wales, Australia. Robert Alfred Driscoll's early struggles 'down under' read almost like a romance. His first pocket money occupation after school hours was as a door to door salesman, selling oranges from a pram and sharing the proceeds with his neighbour who was the orange grower. He learnt he could make money collecting bottles, waste paper and other items, providing him with further funds.

At the age of fourteen, R. A. Driscoll's first real employment was as parcel boy at a local draper's shop. The love of the job led him to rapid promotion, from salesman to window-dresser to assistant manager whilst still in his teens. Then came the big move to progressive stores in Melbourne, with promotions ranging from display manager to buyer. He then moved to Sydney and further success. By his early twenties Mr Driscoll had the wanderlust and travelled to Fiji, the South Seas, Tasmania and Hong Kong.

In 1909, in his mid twenties, he had saved enough money for his fare "£14 steerage" to sail to England. It was a rather daunted young Australian who arrived on British soil. He found himself in London with his cabin trunk and £12 in his pocket and no friends, no home and no job. Employment, which had to be fought for back home, was scarce here too. Mr Driscoll was ill dressed. A "frock coat and silk hat" were the uniform of the day so he bought a second hand hat, borrowed a frock coat and found a job in London as a 'shop-walker' and window-dresser.

R. A. Driscoll moved onwards and upwards. He was employed at John Barker's by Sir Sidney Skinner (who later became Chairman) as a display manager and received great encouragement at the hands of this "merchant prince". Sir Sidney realised he had a genius on his hands who would shortly leave him to double his salary with William Whitelay in London then onto Gooch's in Brompton Road as general manager. This was to seal his reputation as a craftsman in the art of window dressing. He had original ideas and ideals, a dynamic personality and was hardworking. His undoubted ability as a leader soon showed itself. His order of thinking in business was "thoroughness" and being practical. With insight and energy added to his other qualities he was head and shoulders above other men in the same line of business and was bound to come to the fore.

Money was never his first objective. His one and only aim was success. Mr Driscoll inspired and encouraged those working under him, knowing that no business was ever successfully built without the help and co-operation of all employed from the humble errand-boy to buyers and directors.

Kennards' progress became phenomenal from the day R. A. Driscoll joined the board of directors in 1921. Presentation had always been of prime importance and it became clear to William

Kennard that Mr Driscoll's new and previously untried methods of merchandise presentation were successful. He had previously shown real flare when he staged some spectacular displays for the opening of a new store in 1911 by Queen Alexandra. His methods in the previous decade were so revolutionary as to be treated as news by daily national newspapers. By mid 1930s he made the men at Debenham & Freebody, Marshall & Snelgrove and Harvey Nicholls all "shudder as the latest stories of his exploits circulated". Kennards' remarkable development was undoubtedly due to R. A. Driscoll's drive and originality. The store now had a presiding genius. It would also become apparent that he was rather a 'showman' and that there were going to be lots of treats in store.

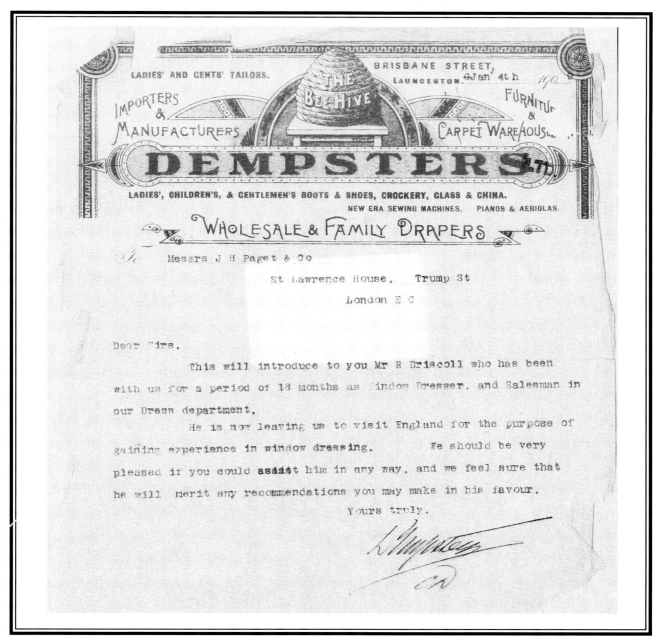

Mr. Driscoll's reference letter dated 1909.

Batchelars

Batchelors decorated for a Royal occasion (the succession to the throne of King George VI and Queen Elizabeth), 1937.

Batchelars was an important store situated at 39-47 North End Croydon (where the Drummond Centre now exists). It was established in 1834 and originally specialised in furnishings, removals and warehousing, owning several large depositories locally which were "heated by hot water and always open for inspection" and were pronounced by insurance companies to be "the best in existence". There were also other depositories in Beckenham and Bromley with offices in London. In its day it was an emporium with a reputation for quality goods and service. It sold furniture in every style and period along with pianos, carpets "British and foreign" and a variety of fabrics for curtains, draperies and coverings. By 1919 its businesses included house-decorators, auctioneers, estate agents, electrical engineers, plumbers and gas fitters.

Before the Second World War Batchelars' 'floor walker' was Mr Ridley. It was usual for a floor or 'shop walker' to personally escort a customer to a seat by the department counter of their choice and make sure they were attended to. Mr Ridley carried out this duty on rare occasions when trade was quiet in the store. This type of service originated from the 'carriage trade'. In times past customers would alight from their carriages outside a shop or store, be met at the main entrance by the principal shop-walker, usually the proprietor, who would escort them into the store. Another shop-walker would be called to assist the customer who would be offered seating on a 'bent-wood' chair, which was the traditional seating for customers in drapery stores and shops. There were usually two or more chairs to each counter. Very little stock was put on show in the early years and customers had the

An interior view of Batchelars' showhouse, c. mid-1930s.

required articles brought to them at the counter and were personally attended to.

Batchelars had quite a remarkable feature in its store and delighted onlookers when they visited the 'show house'. This was constructed in 1930 on the first floor and on view until just after the Second World War when it was converted into offices. The accommodation, of ground and upper storeys, was completed with a front 'garden'. During the store's centenary celebrations "Miss Enid Stamp-Taylor the well known actress and film star" opened the new modern furnished house. Of particular interest that year in the furnishings was the display of two carpets; one used by Queen Victoria at the opening of the Hyde Park Exhibition in 1851 and the other a 16th century Ouchak carpet valued at £1,500. To enhance the celebrations further a 13-year-old "leading pianist of the day" gave daily recitals.

Although Kennards had 'joint control' of Batchelars' premises in 1929, they kept the Batchelars name throughout much of Kennards' ownership. Its high-class reputation was not under estimated as many an advertisement read "The Houses of Kennards and Batchelars".

Above: The traditional 'bentwood' chair, 1905.
Below: A Batchelars' Showcase, c. mid-1930s.

Batchelars, decorated for the Coronation of H.M. Queen Elizabeth II
(note Kennards name upon the fascia), 1953.

Kennards' Arcade

Kennards took advantage of the close proximity of Batchelars and the acquisition of the store (in 1929) enabled the construction of the magnificent main arcade in the mid 1930s, thereby linking the two emporia and affording access to the ground and first floors of both stores. The arcade was built on the site of Hedgis Yard (see map). Hedgis Yard was a public thoroughfare but had restrictions on its use by a pair of lockable gates. The passageway led from North End, alongside J. Lyons and Co. in between and behind the two stores and opened into Grove Place, Grove Cottages, Newton Cottages and also Vine Cottage. Hedgis Yard was named after Thomas Hedgis who resided in Grove Place in 1865 and was a "builder, undertaker and tobacconist". The other cottages housed a shoemaker, blacksmith, a dressmaker and a coach painter among others.

Agreements between Kennards and the County Borough of Croydon between 1933 and 1935 enabled Kennards to redevelop Hedgis Yard. The Borough obtained some land in Frith Road and at the corner of Frith Road and Keeley Road for

Above: Hedgis Yard. Nos. 6–20 were demolished in 1932, c. early 1930s. Below: Kennards' 'bold' Frith Road entrance led to all departments, 1937.

highway improvements. All the cottages, stables and outbuildings were demolished to make way for Kennards to extend to Frith Road and the Frith Road, Keely Road corner. This enabled the covered arcade to run through the depth of the store.

Vista in the main arcade, 1937.

This new arcade enticed shoppers from the public foot-way by "its illumination and tasteful combination of light colours, in pastel shades of mauve, green and cream". Once inside the arcade, from the North End entrance, the public could venture into one or other of the two stores. On each side of the arcade were showcase type windows, framed in bronze and fitted with clipped glazing in various sizes and depths. The pilasters at the entrance to the arcade, panels at intervals, parts of the frieze and the stepped risers beneath the stairway showcases were all faced with Napoleon marble, while the low risers beneath the windows were of black marble.

The arcade had distinct sections. The first was at pavement level. Centrally placed in the front part of this was an entrance to the basement, adjoining which three stanchions provided structural support for the upper storeys, faced with brilliant cut mirrored glass and shallow showcases. In this section of the arcade two kiosks were constructed on either side for use as reception desks in conjunction with any given department, or as temporary mini-sales departments in themselves or showcases for partial open displays. The upper portions of these kiosks could be enclosed at night by revolving shutters. The flooring of this first part was covered with square rubber tiles of marble pattern, within a yard or so of the pavement line, where a threshold of white marble tiles was laid. A short flight of seven stairs led to the second part of the arcade and a further showcase in the same design as the kiosks with a 'stepped' treatment in Napoleon marble beneath the glazed display portion.

More changes to their 'new look' store, 1937.

The other part of the arcade was fitted out with woven furniture and floral decorations and had something of a lounge atmosphere. The floor was of terrazzo, divided into squares and relieved by star designs. On the left, approached by three quadrant shaped steps beneath an illuminated canopy, was a doorway in an illuminated architrave leading to the restaurant on the first floor. A circular daylight afforded maximum lighting for this section and all the windows and showcases had enclosures of quarter-panelled walnut veneer and cross banding and bases of parquetry. A battery of five doors divided the central hall, just described, from the inner vestibule, from which flights of stairs led down to Batchelars on one side and to Kennards on the other.

The arcade, like the remainder of the store, frequently changed its décor and style over the years. By 1937 the main arcade opened and the store stated that it was "the first store in the country to have an arcade street of shops", mostly occupied by small private businesses. In the 1950s it had evolved into an Elizabethan mock Tudor street which continued to accommodate private traders and displayed all sorts of attractions and diversions in the decades to come and are highlighted in Chapter 16.

Kennards' Art-Deco entrance in North End, 1937.

A Guide Around The Store

The automatic central desk. On the first day of the summer sale "over 10,000 cash transactions were handled by the Desk". 1923.

The pre (Second World) war store guide reveals that Kennards opened its doors to the public at 9 am each day (except Sundays). Closing times varied; 6.30 pm on Mondays; 7 pm Tuesdays and Thursdays; 7.30 pm Fridays and 8 pm on Saturdays with half day closing at 1 pm on Wednesdays.

View of part of the dispatch section of the central Cash Desk, c. late 1920s.

Kennards had all the modern features of the day, such as an Automatic Sprinkler and Alarm System, installed throughout the premises as well as a Lamson Pneumatic Tube System. Before the invention of pneumatic tubes there were the Lamson's hollow wooden cash balls, made in the early 1880s. These ran along inclined tracks above each counter. They were replaced by 'overhead railways', supporting cash containers, which resembled miniature cable cars. The containers were impelled along by an assistant who pulled a cord and the containers shot off with a 'ping' on their journeys around the ceilings of a store. They sped about and turned corners and were a delight for children to watch. These were still in use in small town drapers well into the 1950s. Then came the pneumatic tubes, which were in manufacture by 1900. Kennards had 12 of the Lamson automatic belt cash desk stations installed in 1906 and these were added to from time to time.

It was considered "the latest cash service" with an Automatic Central Desk. When a purchase was made the invoice and money was sealed in a tube carrier and sent off from one of the 150 'stations' throughout the store to the Central Desk. The cashiers would empty each tube and replace with receipt and change and return it to the department. A tube carrier could reach the cash desk from the most distant stations in 30 seconds and travelled at speeds of around 25 mph.

On the ground floor an interesting novelty was the newly erected 'signposts' which directed shoppers to the various departments. The 'Foreign Fancy' department (the equivalent of our gift department today) was near the North End main entrance in 1913. Here they sold thousands of articles, mostly imported direct by Kennards. From the "Land of the Lotus" came Japanese china, candlesticks and rose bowls. They sold an endless variety of goods from Vienna, Paris and elsewhere,

ranging from leather bags to fancy clocks. Then came the toys. Kennards alleged themselves to be one of the first of the larger stores to introduce the 'Christmas Toy Fair' and had its first big display of toys in the early 1900s. Also on this floor level could be found soft furnishings, paper patterns, Turkish towels and gramophone records, along with laces, ribbons and trimmings (i.e. Haberdashery) which would be displayed on a counter situated near the main entrance of any store. Although the cash turnover for haberdashery was small it was an expected service.

Top: The Foreign Fancy Department, 1912.

Left: The Foreign Fancy Department (note the Lamson tubes around the ceilings), 1923.

Above: The Toy Bazaar in the Basement, 1912.
Below: The 'trimmings', c. early 1920s.

The Basement displayed sewing machines, bicycles, pianos, portable wireless sets and showrooms of rugs, linoleum, floor coverings, iron-mongery, household utensils and glass and china.

There was also a 'Bargain Basement' (as many stores lower floors became). This was a new innovation, which first appeared in London stores by 1912.

Above: Bags, trunks and basketware in the basement, c. early 1920s.
Below: China and Glass Department, c. early 1920s.

One of the three main staircases (erected in 1880, 1905 and 1922, of which two were dismantled later), c. late 1920s.

The first floor, which was approached via the grand staircase, housed the private directors' offices and children's and ladies' clothing. "Realistic dummies" were used to display the latest fashion, with mirrors in evidence everywhere where numerous curtained recesses acted as changing rooms. By the

Top: The first floor Robe Showroom, c. 1920s.
Bottom: Mr. Harding (Director and General Manager) checking stock in the store, c. mid-1930s.

middle of the 1930s the store incorporated an 18 cubicle ladies' hairdressing salon representing "the last word in toilet luxury". This was housed on the first floor along with a small Travel Bureau, which sold coach and London theatre tickets. This Bureau was a novel feature for its time. (The Bureau later moved to the main arcade.) Also on this level could be found the lost property, account and club departments, cloakrooms, a café and a lending library. This new library was decorated in cream, black and scarlet. It was to extend over the next few years and Dennis Wheatley the writer and actor and author Howard Spring opened, on separate occasions, the new 'Mudie's' and 'Sundial' library. The library had "a service of over two million books", of which 3.000 were permanently in stock. Customers could borrow 'Class B' or the latest 'Class A' books at a small charge. It had a 'Juvenile section' with special low-built shelves and an experienced librarian in attendance. One could also recline in the reading, writing or rest room, which was available for the customer's convenience. The top floor was devoted entirely to the Counting House.

Top: The Perfumery Department, c- mid 1930s.
Above: Egg, cucumber and tomato masks, mud packs and ankle reducing treatments were all available in the Beauty Parlour, 1940.

Above: The Beauty Parlour interior showing the changing cubicles, 1940.
Below: Kennards' Library, 1935.

Above: The Counting House, c. early 1920s.
Below: A main aisle in the Cash and Carry Department, 1932.

Above: Cottons, Prints and Fancy Linens Department, with numerous bentwood chairs for customers' comfort, 1905.

Left: Mantle and Costume Showroom, 1913.

Left: Down Quilt and Curtain Department, 1913.

Below: More fashion and finery (note the articles hanging from the ceiling), c. early 1900s.

Top left: The Bedding Department, c. early 1920s.

Bottom left: A casual display of hats, c. early 1900s.

Bottom right: "In a Garden of Roses". This theme was carried throughout the store during Opening Week, 1923.

Top: The opening ceremony (possibly the three floors which were added to the small block at the rear of the store), 1923.

Left: Women's Hats. There was also a 'Kids Lids' (children's hats) department. c. 1920s.

Above: One of the Furnishing Departments, c. early 1920s.
Below: Another spacious and stylish department in 1923.

Above: The Art and Needlework Department, c. early 1920s.
Below: Linens, 1923.

Above: Another view of the Foreign Fancy Department, 1923.
Below: Modern Merchandising, c. early 1920s.

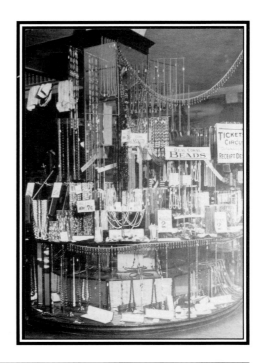

Top: This display secured the first prize in the Wolsey All England Window Display competition in 1921.

Left: A close up of a mannequin from the Wolsey window display.

Right: Beads and Stationery, c. early 1920s.

There was also one acre of workrooms and an extensive garage. The Cash and Carry Store built in 1932 as a new extension facing Frith Road comprised 50 sub-departments spaced out in 'island units', which operated on a "self-service promotional system", selling varied merchandise including women's wear and fashion accessories. This ran as a quick service/fixed price department selling to a "popular class of trade". The external facade of this extension was fitted with a canopy with illuminated lettering. This was one of the first British store canopies. Courtney Pope & Co., Ltd. and Samuel Elliott & Sons (Reading) Ltd. were responsible for the shop-front and illuminated canopy and all interior equipment. Kennards'

architects, George Baines & Son, carried out many reconstruction schemes over the years. This 'finish' gave the department a distinct entity as "Kennards' Cash and Carry Stores".

By 1935 Kennards' great provision market on the lower ground floor contained a huge cold storage room to further guarantee freshness to its seasonal produce and they had fully extended their store to Frith Road and Keeley Road. With 150 departments, a new car park in Keeley Road that accommodated 100 cars and an adjoining "quick snack counter for the convenience of owner-drivers and customer's chauffeurs", Kennards were now occupying a ten-acre site which afforded much more valuable display space.

Kennards' Art-Deco entrance in Drummond Road and its car park, c. late 1930s.

Above: Kennards and Batchelars in North End, c. late 1930s.
Below: One of the first shops to open in the new main arcade, 1937.

They were skilful in their presentations of 'a shop within a shop'. By 1937 small private businesses operated within the main arcade such as Messrs Bunn, whose previous premises had been acquired by the local Council as street widening was being considered. Individual shops that operated in the store and arcade paid their own staff and displayed their own goods but the store took a percentage of the sales. Individual agreements with each Company were drawn up.

Highly professional and 'City' in atmosphere at Kennards' Thrift Bank, 1937.

Kennards did not favour any form of instalment credit trading at this time, but it had a Thrift Bank. Customers received a 7½% interest on condition that monies were spent in the store. It had its own laundry and combined it with a laundry service for customers. Table linen, kitchen cloths, lavatory towels and even nappies, which were collected, washed, sterilised and delivered back to customers was part of the service! The store boasted of a world record in shirt laundering. An American trade paper of 1937 quoted a 30 minute laundering service and it prompted Kennards to advertise to its customers that they could launder a customer's shirt in 15 minutes.

Above: The 'Dogs Toggery', 1937. Below: Kennards' dog boarding kennels at Godstone, Surrey, c. late 1930s.

Credit must go to its more unusual departments throughout the store. A 'dog's toggery' department, completely self contained, sold anything from baskets to leads. There was also a puppy market and dogs beauty parlour. Kennards also had dog-boarding kennels in Godstone, Surrey which included a collection and delivery service for customers' pets.

The Tudor Cafe opened in 1914, c. late 1920s.

Other departments included an Oil Baize shop (oil baize was a thick plastic oilcloth which could be bought by the yard; a washable and durable table covering material), a Herb shop and a Dutch Bulb Shop, which contained over one million Dutch and English bulbs. There was also a children's 'barber's shop', a self-service grocery and a 'Karpenter's Korner'. Places of refreshment were many in the 1930s such as the Sundae Bar, the main restaurant (which could accommodate 600 diners at one sitting) and the 'Blue Room', a staff restaurant and also a 'serve yourself' café. The store also had two 'open spaces' in the shape of exhibition halls on the ground floor, available for exhibition purposes and staging of special events.

One of several places for refreshment in the store, c. mid-1930s.

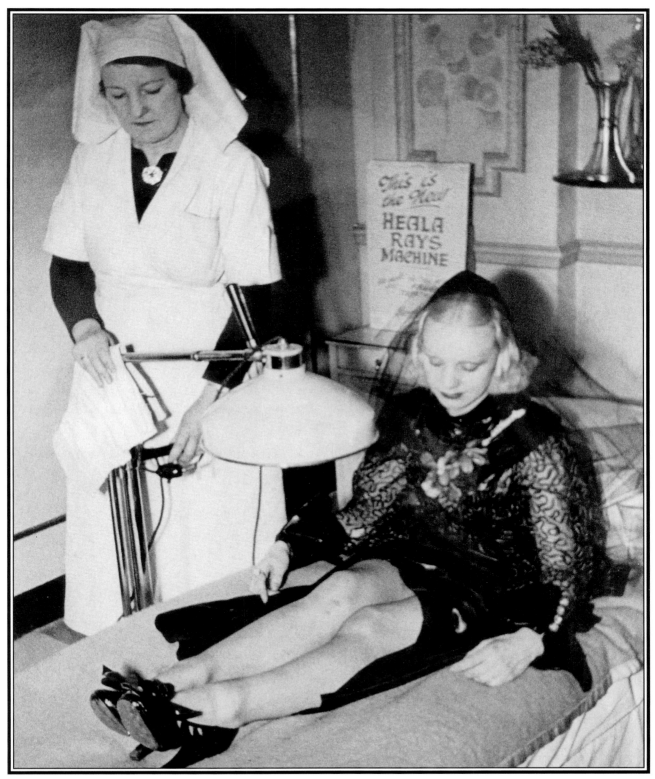

'Mlle Veronica' was a regular user of the Heala Ray machine, 1937.

Customers afflicted with corns could leave them behind at Kennards; this was quite separate from the chiropody parlour. There were an Osteopathy Parlour and a Heala Health Centre made available to staff and customers alike. The heala ray machine was invented by Mr W. T. Russell. He was a personal friend of Mr Driscoll who had heard of its remarkable healing properties and decided his staff and customers could benefit from it. It was installed in the beauty salon and supervised by a qualified nurse. Kennards negotiated for the selling rights and sold many of these machines in its store. They claimed that it relieved all rheumatic ailments and skin troubles and more, and reported that the store's absenteeism had reduced to less than 5%. Dental repairs were also carried out and deaf aids could be purchased.

Mr Jackson was a regular visitor to Kennards. He was a "famous manipulative specialist" who gave daily demonstrations and carried out "successful treatments" in cases of dislocation, arthritis, stomach troubles, headaches etc. There was 'Doctor N'Gai' the Mystery Man or 'Great White Witch Doctor' who could perhaps cure one's ills more effectively; he could be found in the piano department accompanied by the store's pianist playing all the latest hits!

A view around the store in mid to late 1940s reveals scenes just as bizarre as the previous decade. As in 1939, Kennards still retained a 'Phrenology Consulting Room' where one could have one's head read. This involved a study of the shape of a person's skull, the theory being that this could indicate the character and mental powers of the person studied. Palms could be read too, by hands dipped in a black substance and then pressed onto large white sheets of paper. The results could then be studied and predictions made. In the chiropody department one could also have one's verrucas treated – two feet for the price of one.

Ida Santerelli and her girls in the main restaurant. The organ (installed in 1933) was reported to be "the first to be built in the restaurant of any store in London", c. mid-1930s.

Ida Santerelli and her girls with one of the animal 'exhibits' in the restaurant, c. mid-1930s.

Customers requiring refreshment after their shopping spree could visit the main restaurant and hear Dorothy Marno's Bohemian Orchestra or the resident band Ida Santerelli and her girls playing their instruments under the palm trees on the stage. The stage was at the far end of the restaurant, in front of a pair of golden gates. Between the gates a small church type pipe organ (removed from the Scala Cinema opposite and installed in Kennards in 1933) played with the orchestra on Saturdays. Daphne Kelf, the "celebrated West-End vocalist and cabaret star", who also featured in Kennards' fashion parades as a "singing mannequin", sang "light songs" and on rare occasions was accompanied by Mr Driscoll in a duet. (Daphne Kelf became Mr Driscoll's second wife.) Whilst drinking tea from Kennards' bone china teacups, decorated in red polka dots with gold rims, customers could enjoy various forms of entertainment. There were

'Pharos & Farina' the two famous quick fire telepathists or 'Kushorney – the Mystery Mind', the "most sensational mind reader" who entertained during their lunch and tea. Daily cabaret shows featuring 'The Sparklettes' and tea dances were regular features held in the restaurant in the 1940s.

There was also help for harassed mothers. Kennards provided, free of a charge, a "pram park". This was probably situated on the first floor of Batchelars store (now under Kennards control) as they directed customers "in the road leading to the zoo".

The signposts were replaced by a tall man dressed in a long coat and peaked hat. He stood on a rostrum, just inside the main store entrance and directed customers to the different departments. On one occasion, when no one enquired directions of him, he said in a slightly exasperated voice: "Ask me, ask me, why don't you ask me?"

One sales assistant described working conditions in the 1950s with "staff wearing black or navy and white outfits, working in cramped areas" and "when the cash tills malfunctioned multiple purchases were calculated mentally or using pencil and paper". The scene to the entrance of 'Department 40, the Foreign Fancy', near the front main entrance, sported "gold coloured swing doors, art nouveau-style. Square counters crowded with an exotic array of goods. A robed Indian who spoke no English, held sway over a perfume and fancy goods stall against the wall by the entrance". Cardboard scenery in odd corners in the departments portrayed "bright summer skies, palm trees and flowering shrubs which harboured exotic birds in far-away locations by the sea".

When the store was about to close for the night Kennards played a Gracie Fields recording over the public address system, which became more crackled and scratched as the years went by called "Now is the hour, when we must say goodbye".

An Oddfellows Centenary Dinner in the main restaurant. It was "Croydon's most popular rendezvous for lunch and tea". 1947.

Above: Kennards Supermarket, 1959.
Below: Kennards celebrate Britain's Festival Year and their own successful progress, 1951.

The Kennardians

A. J. Smith
Buyer Hardware Dept. &
Chairman of 'Warwick House'

Mr. Smith

W. Roy Driscoll
General Manager
Kennards Wimbledon

A. Harding
Director & General Manager

W. Dudley Kennard
Director and Company Secretary

The employees of Kennards called themselves 'Kennardians' after being portrayed in fine fashion in the monthly edition of 'Kennards Gazette'. The journal was "the official organ of the WHAA (Warwick House Athletic Association). This magazine commenced publication in 1933 but ceased at the outbreak of the Second World War. Although Kennards depicted some of its staff in caricature fashion in "Our Portrait Gallery" in the journal, there is no doubt that Kennards was proud of its staff, who were loyal, conscientious and upheld the store's traditions and values and were held in high regard. Typical entries are as follows:

Miss Winckworth joined the store in 1914 and was employed as a Buyer of Mantles, Costumes and Coats. She held the 'Buyer's Cup' on numerous occasions, along with "many other rewards and trophies during her career at Kennards, never surpassed by any other employee". Her hobbies were dancing, tennis and skating. Added to this "a loveable disposition and a smile for everybody, then take a peep at her caricature and you have Miss Winckworth just as she is".

Meet Miss Sibery, who joined Kennards in

1917. Loyalty and hard work rewarded her and she was appointed Buyer for the Millinery Department. The artificial flower section "flourished under her buyership". Two hobbies gave her intense pleasure; "a walk in the country and dusting thousands of hats a day in the store, with the help of the little brush seen in this picture".

Mr Vaughan started business life as a "lather" boy in a local barber's shop, progressing to many Mayfair hairdressers. He worked at Hyde Park Hotel and is said to have "shaved and trimmed the hair of half the potentates (leaders) of Europe and

The "Kennardians". 'Lifelike' caricatures of some of the staff, c. mid-1930s.

the East". He became "a specialist in ladies hairdressing in Harrods and the favourite barber of many leading actresses of the day". Mr Vaughan spent the war years in France, "bobbing in and out of the trenches to shave every other famous General you have ever heard of, and the Tommies too, at a franc a time". He joined Kennards in 1925 to open and manage the hairdressing department and beauty parlour.

Miss Ganderton was "a success from the start". Upon leaving school she worked as an "unpaid, apprenticed cashier in the restaurant" for William Whiteley in London. She went on to Gordon Selfridge's store in Oxford Street and became his restaurant cashier on the "very day he opened shop" in 1909. In the fullness of time she joined Kennards who had "nothing but praise" as she took on the role of restaurant manageress in 1926. Her hobbies "a nice book, a nice fire and a nice box of chocolates".

Mr Cawte started business 'in the trade' as an Indentured Apprentice. He gained experience in "workshops and the selling side" and became a traveller or "Mercantile Tourist". Next we find him in the carpet department in William Whitelay's store. In 1914 he is in hottest India and during his military duties there he was able to see at first hand the manufacture of carpets in Bangalore, Agra and Amritsaw where he witnessed interesting sights such as the convoys of camels unloading carpets in Peshawar market. Mr Cawte returned to Britain and peacetime. In 1927 he joined Kennards and became buyer for the carpet and floor coverings department.

Mr Nichols started his apprenticeship in 'Drapery' in Bristol. He became a "rolling stone" to obtain as much and as varied experience as possible. He secured positions in many British stores as a buyer. His last appointments were as buyer for the linen departments in stores in Liverpool, Manchester and Birmingham, "thus becoming the largest buyer of this merchandise in the retail trade". Mr Nichols joined Kennards in 1929 as Buyer and was promoted to Merchandise Manager of all the Household Departments. His hobbies were tennis and gardening and his habit was "toys with his tie". It was said that he wore out more ties than all the rest of the Buyers put together.

Mr Beretta was "born within the sound of Bow Bells and very proud of it". His father was Italian, hence his intriguing name. Mr Beretta decided "whilst still in short trousers that the sports trade looked a promising career as any, so served his time at the bench". To "young Beretta", all the glamour of the sports trade seemed to be on the selling side, but scope, like selling space, was limited. "Half an acre of billiard tables, bicycles and even a miniature golf course came into his scheme of things". So, in 1929, he opened a sports department in Kennards, where he sold every kind of indoor and outdoor sports equipment one could think of, from golf ball 'repaints' to caravans.

Mr Grantham stood "two yards and three inches in his socks". He was educated at the Choir School of St John's College in York and served a five year indentured apprenticeship at a Military, Clerical and Civilian Outfitters and Tailors. He gained Buyers experience at various stores and went through the Great War as Dispatch Rider in the Royal Air Force. Mr Grantham secured a position at Kennards in 1931 as Buyer of Men's and Boy's Outfitting and Clothing Department, "increasing the turnover and size of departments out of all knowledge".

Mr Edwards "heard the bugle call in 1914 and saw four years war service". He became a prominent member of the famous 'Ricardos' Concert Party at Arras Theatre, France. He was next found touring England as a professional singer when he embarked on a commercial career. He became a central buyer of haberdashery and other fancy goods, which entailed travel of about 800 miles each week with regular visits to the Continent. He joined Kennards in 1932 to manage the newly opened Cash and Carry Store.

Mr Pumphrey wrote of himself in 'Our Portrait Gallery' in the 1936s in-house Gazette that after his Trinity College education in Eastbourne, Sussex he was "apprenticed to the Rag Trade" for three years. He gained experience and studied display methods in various stores around the South East of England and central London such as Chiesman's of Lewisham and Derry & Toms in Kensington as "head window dresser (Display Manager, as a title, was then unknown)". Two of his favourite hobbies were "letting my staff know how much better I was than they are at their age" and "dodging commercial travellers".

From Cradle to Grave

Russel School 'Ballards', Addington, Surrey, 1924.

The origin of the Warehousemen & Clerk's Schools is complex, but is fully recorded by the publication of the "Royal Russell School – A History" by an ex-schoolmaster, S. Hopewell, for those wishing to delve further into its history.

The 'orphan schools' enterprise originated in 1853, when a group of clerks who worked in London wholesale warehouses decided to assist the widow and her young family of one of their colleagues who had died. Victorian attitudes differed from those today, with education and welfare being sadly neglected.

The clerks' farsighted action led to the founding of a charity which enfolded the whole of their trade and encouraged active interest and support from all quarters. From the care of one family the charity developed to support hundreds of "poor and necessitous orphan children". At first the orphans were educated in a school in New Cross, but increase in pupils led to the Committee seeking new premises so they built their own school at Russell Hill in Purley, the first of two schools.

It was opened in 1866 and housed 150 girls and 60 junior boys and was initially supported and financed solely by the textile trade and flourished until after the First World War. The school was so successful it became over-crowded with 327 pupils, so funds were sought to buy a new site and create a separate boy's school as a 'Textile Trade War Memorial'. The new school, established in 1921, was situated in a mansion house on the 'Ballards' estate, once a country residence in Addington, at the top of the Shirley hills. The school developed, new buildings were erected in 1924 and accommodated 150 senior boys. In 1963 the school was officially named the Royal Russell School. By 1972 it no longer served the trade alone for only 70 out of its 400 pupils were 'foundationers'. There had been several 'Debenham Scholarships' (Kennards' successor) for the study of foreign languages and one of the many benefactors commemorated in the school buildings is William Debenham.

Kennards called Russell Hill "our own school" and one of many party visits was organised to view both the schools in late 1933. The store ardently supported the schools and encouraged its staff to do likewise with whist drives, dances and the 'Purley penny league float'. Kennards encouraged its employees to give weekly voluntary subscriptions towards the fund. There was also a 'Lorry fund'. A lorry full of furniture destined for the school would initially drive around the different firm's premises and employees were asked to throw their spare cash into the lorry. Kennards continued its support when pupils set forth into the world, whatever or wherever the place. The store supplied new clothing free of charge ranging from underwear to shoes and coats.

At the turn of the 20th century most of the ex-scholars moved into the business of the Warehousemen, Clerk's & Draper's as apprentices. Out of 20 of Russell Hill's first 'school leavers' 11 joined

Kennards' Sales Assistants, c. mid-1930s.

firms that supported the school. Apprentices usually 'lived in', as this was the most common form of shop employment. In 1907 there were 450,000 shop assistants that lived in. Kennards was one of many firms which had accommodation provided for its employees. There were a few single rooms on the top floor of its department store and further staff accommodation, bought or rented at different times in Leonard Road, Park Hill Road and Wellesley Road in Croydon was available for employees. Staff only ventured home during their annual leave or Bank holidays and had to be 'in' by 10 pm with lights out by 11 pm and doors locked. The sales girls shared three to a room and the buyers had their own rooms. The housekeeper had her own suite of rooms for herself and her family. Social life may not have been so stunted as one imagines, for a 'late-pass' could be obtained if the employee attended a dance or theatre. The locking of premises was abandoned at the outbreak of the Second World War because of the hazards of air raids.

The sales assistants employed were carefully vetted for speech and good character and many would seek to climb the ladder to reach the ultimate post of buyer. They were continually trained in

The radio-active corset had "an enthusiastic reception on the British market", 1937.

order to keep abreast of outside competition. One such area of trade in 1937 was in corsetry. The store held "special corset fitting weeks". Mr Driscoll recognised the corset department as being in the "front rank as a profit making investment" and had staff trained to "know their subject technically" and encouraged them to attend a series of talks on the subject. The London County Council arranged the talks, which covered design, manufacture, surgical corsetry, stock control, publicity and salesmanship at the Barrett Street Trade School in Oxford Street, London. The new corset department serviced by trained staff would "enhance corset sales". The growing alertness on the part of the customer demanded a higher-grade selling service and the store was aware of the "increased style consciousness" of its customers.

This is a mere glimpse into one area of staff training and employees were rewarded well if their efforts bore fruit. In more modern times firm's sales assistants were sent to Draper's Summer Schools to learn the theory and practise of retail salesmanship. There was also a London County Council Trade School for Girls. These are just two such examples of training opportunities. Mr Driscoll also believed in the educational influence of travel and as early as 1937 impressive inducements such as trips to America and Paris were given as incentive awards. There were presentations of cups such as the Challenge cup, the Buyer's Gift cup, a biannual competition, which encouraged the buyers to put on the best show of merchandise and to reach the highest target on the first day of the sales. There was also a November Handicap (sales

The Grand Staircase, c. mid-1930s.

race) cup including cash prizes which were the employees rewards. In 1938 the firm instituted a 'Banner of Merit' monthly award which included a five guinea cheque (around £5.25p today, which was about two weeks wages in those days) to the department that showed the biggest increase in turnover. Presentations were awarded to the winner on the main staircase in front of all the employees and amidst loud applause the recipient would descend the staircase proudly waving the banner. Staff meetings, which most employees attended, were also held on the grand main staircase. The Board of Directors stood at the top and thanks were often showered upon the managers, buyers and staff for their loyalty and good work in "furthering the success of our wonderful store".

There were presentations of other cups too on its sports and social side. Kennards had its own sports ground in Pampisford Road, South Croydon for staff and management use. The highlight of the year was the annual sports day, which included 300 entries for 31 events. One such day in mid 1930s sported one-mile relays against the United Dairies and pillow fights. Mr William Kennard, Mr & Mrs Rex Kennard, Mr & Mrs Dudley Kennard, Mr & Mrs Driscoll and Mr & Mrs Harding were present to enjoy the events and many side shows and attractions were put on for the day. The sports

Mrs. Cresswell, employed for 31 years, "delighted thousands of guests in her capacity as Banqueting Chef at Kennards" and assisted the restaurant staff in making hundreds of packed lunches for the staff annual outings. She was presented with flowers on her 65th birthday. Mr Huxstead, Restaurant Manager and his wife stand left of Mrs. Cresswell, 1962.

Kennards' Restaurant Staff in North End await their coaches for the Staff Annual Outing, c. 1950s.

and social circle also included tennis, men's and women's hockey, football, cricket, athletics and weekly swimming sessions at the Croydon Baths in Scarbrook Road. A dramatic society, a health and culture club along with a hiking section and many other activities were catered for. There were also The William Kennard and The Driscoll Autumn Golf cups, cycling, model engineering and table tennis cups.

Its Women's League of Health & Beauty was held in the staff restaurant every Friday evening where a two-hour session of "elementary health, medium health, elementary tap and cabaret and skipping" took place. Cricket matches were held against the Sydenham Tradesmen and the Royal Air Force teams from Kenley along with swimming galas competing against Allders and table tennis matches in the South London Business House Tournament with Kennards finishing runners-up to Messrs Bentalls.

The annual staff outings are the most well remembered social occasions. The store advertised in the Croydon Times to "shop early" as "this coming Wednesday is the staff annual outing and the store will be closed for the entire day". Staff, numbering between 800 to 1,000, boarded no fewer than 30 coaches in July 1937 and travelled to Hastings for their day's trip. A convoy of coaches departed from North End each year, usually to the South coast. Coaches were lettered A to Z with separate coaches for the kitchen staff, cleaners, managers and visitors. The outings were at the firm's expense with free packed lunches for every employee and "pocket money for the younger folk". The outing was filmed and shown at the Davis Theatre that particular year and were just as impressive in decades to come.

Kennards produced its own in-house Gazette and further insight into this journal is covered in Chapter 9. There was also a junior monthly magazine called Dolphin for children aged between 7-14.

It was not surprising to find large numbers of staff in any firm's employment serving from upwards of 15 to 45 years. Men who still worked at 70 years of age or more were not uncommon and a 50 years' ceremony service was not infrequent. One such employee was George Langford. He was Kennards' oldest employee who originally worked for Tom Batchelar, founder of the great local emporium Batchelars Ltd. George Langford was initially employed as a coachman and recalls a time in 1887 when "as many as 27 to 30 horses were kept by the company, working a full six days each week". Round about 'Quarter Day', when the rush of orders was always very heavy, Batchelars had to obtain extra horses to help out with deliveries. George recalled seeing as many as 100 horses and carts waiting to be loaded outside the store at one particular time. George, employed by Batchelars on one month's trial, was informed that if he proved suitable he might be offered a permanent position at the end of that period. George remained in this 'position' long after Kennards took over Batchelars. When George celebrated his 50th anniversary with the store and was due for annual holiday leave he said: "Before I go to the seaside, I think I shall make it my business to ask the firm if they are satisfied with my work during my 'trial' and whether it is their intention to place me on the permanent staff"!

Kennards also helped when its employees retired. Mr Harding, the general manager appealed to the staff to dig deeper into their pockets for the weekly collection to the "Linen & Woollen Drapers' Institution & Cottage Homes", the "oldest Benevolent Institution in our trade" he quoted, stating that "one of the greatest liabilities to our particular trade is old age". The charity was founded in 1832 as a benevolent fund for the needy and incorporated the linen drapers, silk-mercers, hosiers, haberdashers and lace makers trades. The idea for the cottage homes came from James, the elder son of James Marshall (founder of Marshall & Snelgrove). He conceived the philanthropic idea of forming the Linen & Woollen Drapers' Cottage Homes for the retired folk of the trade. On the death of his father, James gave a portion of his family's 1,000 acre estate 'Goldbeater Farm' at Mill Hill in London and financed the construction of the main buildings and some cottages in 1898.

In 1935 Mr Driscoll was elected as 'President of the Appeal' and attended the 103rd annual banquet of the Linen and Woollen Drapers' Institution and Cottage Homes at the Grosvenor House Hotel in Park Lane, London. He thanked his team of buyers, directors and staff for their wonderful support as they had help raise over 500 guineas to build a cottage. Mr Driscoll not only appealed to Kennards but arranged luncheons in business centres throughout the country and invited local drapers highlighting the need for finance for building more cottages and believed the "spoken word" far more effective in his appeals. A total of just over £22,000 was raised and was one of the greatest and proudest days of his life.

The Cottage Homes exist today. Mill Hill covers 16 acres with approximately 150 cottages and is now one of three residential centres in the UK with another planned for Liverpool. Whilst still caring for the retired people from the retail trade its services have greatly expanded. It helps those currently working in the "shop and store" and gives assistance across a spectrum of needs. In 1998 the charity celebrated 50 years of Royal patronage. Her Majesty Queen Elizabeth II is Patron of the Cottage Homes.

The Right Reverend The Lord Bishop of Croydon dedicating and blessing a 'Home' endowed by Kennards, 1950. (Far right: A. Harding, Director and General Manager)

Kennards' Gazette

The in-house Gazettes which were published from 1933 to 1939 unfold many stories of the store and afford a glimpse into the hearts and minds of the management.

In jest Kennards stated that the journal was "the unofficial organ of scandal, tittle-tattle and gossip relating to managers, buyers and staff of Kennards". It was published "solely for the purpose of fostering and promoting the social welfare of every member of the Association". The Gazette covered many facets, ranging from 'society gossip', to reports on 'Warwick House', its sports and social club situated in Pampisford Road, South Croydon. News on Kennards' sister store in Wimbledon; short stories, fact and fiction, jokes and poetry as well as information on their staff annual outings and "messages from the management" all had their place in this monthly magazine to keep the staff fully informed and uplifted in spirit.

The following small selection, taken from the Gazette, gives a flavour of the times and the people of this period and more than hints at the relationship between management and staff.

From W. H. Kennard – Chairman – July 1933

"This first issue of Kennards' Gazette is another of those signs I very much like to see. Signs that we are all becoming more and more of a business "family"; a closely-knit, self-contained unit of the general community working together for the common good. I shall look forward with great interest to the publication of the Gazette and am quite prepared to find that the "Family" is as strong on the literary side as it is on the business side. I expect the Editor will add "Chairman" to my name at the top of this message. If he does I do not want you to take this as written by the Chairman of our Company, but by plain Mr William, the name by which I have been known for nearly half a century by the 'Kennard Family'. Mrs William joins me in wishing every success to the new venture. Good luck to you all".

PATS ON THE BACK

Mr Jacobs – A comparatively new member of the team. A silent worker! We suspect from his knowledge of provisions that he made a very early start in the Trade. Probably dabbled in condensed milk as a baby, followed later by "pinching" mother's currants, raisins and other dainties. Knew how to get "Mother's stock down", but not quite so successful with his own. However, he is a great worker! SPECIAL NOTE – Unless stock is reduced before the next issue of this Journal, a "kick in the pants" will be administered instead of a pat on the back".

A special PAT ON THE BACK for Mr Gilchrist (Soft Furnishing Department) for 24 years loyal

"Mr. & Mrs. William"
The founder's son and daughter-in-law, c. late 1930s.

service to the Firm, and at the same time 21 years devoted service to an invalid wife. Bravo, Gilchrist! You have earned a rest – your business hours in future will be 1 pm to 6 pm on your full Salary".

THE WAY OF A CUSTOMER IN A STORE
He prefers to turn right rather than left.

How to sell things in a store. A few hints by Dr Donald A. Laid, head of the "psychology department" of Colgate University, Toledo. July 1936. "Goods displayed in neat and unbroken stacks do not sell as readily as the same goods in a jumbled heap. Three out of four retail customers want to make right turns instead of a left in a store, and they want to make turns about every twenty feet. The average man will look first at something that is coloured red, then at green, then at orange. He looks at purple last. His attention shifts about every two seconds except when he is especially interested. Goods sell better when there is only a small quantity on display."

THE CUSTOMER
(With acknowledgements to Annette Wilson of Stagg & Russell)

*"How right, how absolutely "Right" the customer
        must be
If she says firmly "Black is White", we humbly
        must agree
We show her this, we show her that, our
        merchandise describing*

*We smile or bow when answered "flat" and bear her
        with deriding
We give her money back and change the goods she's
        worn to pieces
We sell a gown and then arrange a credit if it creases
We write her letters now and then, apologise for
        sending
The small account she owes us when we wish her to
        keep spending
The staff are all required to speak politely in
        replying
When she says "Miss", they quickly ask the
        merchandise she's buying
She patronises them "Poor things", she sometimes
        says in pity
"They look worn out", and then she brings her
        purchase back all 'bitty'
For since the "Modern Rules of Trade" by Gordon
        Selfridge written
Were in the general Press displayed, we've all been
        badly bitten
The customer has learnt the way to claim her will as
        rightful
And grows more righteous every day, in truth she's
        simply FRIGHTFUL"!*

Kennards' Sister Stores

Kennards' 'sister store' in Wimbledon. A queue for stockings. "Nine hundred customers served in 2 hrs". 1949.

Records reveal that Mr Driscoll was "allowed by Debenhams" (Kennards' successor) "to buy his own store at Wimbledon", but to "use the Kennards' name". This was purchased in 1931 and the Kennards' Gazette of the 1930s affectionately referred to it as its "sister store".

It was originally a John Lewis store (no connection with the large chain store) at 33-37 The Broadway, Wimbledon and was initially a ground floor establishment only, occupying a prominent corner position with two inviting corner entrances, linked by an arcade and having display windows on three frontages. It was reconstructed a year later by the same firms that the Croydon store used. A further storey and new internal features were added in later years. By 1936 the store operated under the direction of Mr Driscoll's two sons Desmond and

Roy and "Mr Roy" became the General Manager.

Although the Wimbledon store did not compare in statue to that of its Croydon counterpart and very little is recorded, it played its part in both business and leisure and received loyal support. The store survived until the early 1950s when it was sold.

Pressures on traders during the Second World War brought demise for many businesses, owing to shortages and bomb damage. Between 1943-1945 Debenhams purchased two stores under the Kennards name, one in Redhill, Surrey and the other in Staines, Middlesex. Very little is known about the latter and although named Kennards the store operated under Debenhams' directorship.

The Redhill store opened in 1946 and was formerly Chalmers garage workshop, situated at

Above: A corner view of the Wimbledon store to purchase stockings, 1949.
Below: A queue outside Kennards' Redhill Store which opened in 1946. Reigna, Wards and Chandlers premises were later incorporated into the store. The temporary shop front was later replaced. 1946.

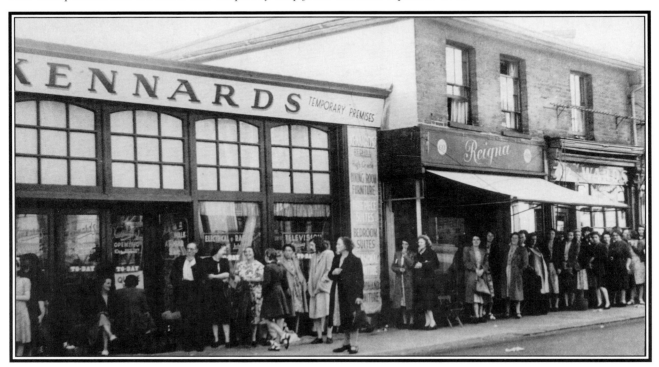

52-60 High Street and sat on a triangular plot. It was a "general drapers and fashion specialists", dealing in fashions, fancy goods, furnishings, carpets, household, electrical and radio goods, including bedding and boasted a small restaurant, with a small upper section on the first floor. It closed in the early 1960s due to redevelopment of the High street.

Top: Kennards' queue continued along the pavement to Chalmers petrol station. 1946.
Right: Chalmers supplied Kennards of Redhill with their first furniture van, a Ford 7V. c. mid-1940s.

Above: Kennards of Redhill, with its new shop front, c. early 1950s.

Right: A new balcony and show department in the Redhill store, 1954.

Below: R. A. Driscoll also opened his own store in Hove, Sussex, at the junction with Church Road/ Ventnor Villas. c. late 1940s.

Are You Being Served Madam?

The time worn phrase "What can we do for you today Madam?" often accompanied by much washing of the hands with invisible soap had no place at Kennards. One was at liberty to roam the store, view exhibits, delight in the store's celebrities and entertainment, whether it was in the arcade, restaurant or the sales floor and with no obligation to buy.

Whilst the customers sauntered around the store, teams of buyers, out of the 50 employed by Kennards, scoured Britain's mills and factories in search of bargains to enhance the reputation of the business. It boasted "up to date stocks" and surplus stocks from manufacturers "successful seasons" which resulted in cheap purchases for the store.

Buying bankrupt stock from various large department stores was quite commonplace for Kennards. In 1928 it purchased the whole stock of Sainsbury's Drapery stores in Lewisham. The size of stock was four times that of Kennards and was purchased for £23.000. In 1937 the entire stock of its North End neighbour Rowbotham (Drapers) worth £34.000, was bought for £19.000. Nineteen firms tendered for the stock. Kennards informed the local press that it took 50 vans 48 hours to complete and convey the stock to its store and that it was "the greatest stock sale in the history of Croydon". A Women's Wear News article reported Kennards with "a record first day with 60.000 transactions represented the highest trading record in the store's history with 58.000 customers". Two weeks intensive preparation during which time buyers and staff worked day and night to ticket 340,000 odd articles – anything from safety pins to fashionable gowns and coats. Kennards not only bought the stock but also managed to find employment for a good number of the 100 saleswomen made unemployed by Rowbotham's closure.

'Streets of Adventure' was another idea to advertise the store's goods. This originated in 1919

Another purchase by Kennards, 1928.

Above: Kennards' delivery vans, c. 1930s.
Below right: Kennards' exhibition stands at the Crystal Palace Show, c. mid-1930s.

by the Church Street and Surrey Street traders, the 'Croydon & District Trader's Association' and was an annual event from the 1920s in an effort to give financial aid to the Croydon General Hospital. Kennards' display floats travelled around the local vicinity completing their journey in Wandle Park and other shops also participated.

In the early 1930s 'Olympia' came to Kennards with 50 demonstration stands taking up a large part of the lower ground floor. These displayed umbrella re-covering, mat making by blind ex-service men, the making of fabric gloves and a "36 hour mattress re-making service" amongst others.

In this same decade the store secured the largest space at the 'South London Exhibition' at Crystal Palace for many of its exhibits ranging from displays of general merchandise to a 'livestock department' where a selection of pedigree dogs was shown. Working looms demonstrated the making of silk stockings and men's pyjamas along with the popular fashion shows for which Kennards were renowned. One thousand seating accommodation was provided for those wishing to view and purchase.

A Kennards' sports display stand at the Crystal Palace exhibition, c. mid-1930s.

*Kennards' fashion show at the Crystal Palace.
A. Harding (Director and General Manager) holds his son's hand. 1936.*

Miss Gladys Wood the "Cotton Beauty Queen of Britain" combined beauty with business and visited the store in 1935. Her mission in her year of office was to stimulate British cotton sales. Kennards held a 'Lancashire Cotton Week' and gave a helping hand to industry.

*More fashion in the store,
c. mid-1930s.*

Kennards' 'in store' fashion parade. One of many. 1937.

Thousands of factory bargains from "the great mills in the North", c. mid-1930s.

Advertising the Buyer's Gift Week by the main front entrance in North End, c. early 1930s.

Kennards' own representatives travelled thousands of miles in search of cheap lines. On one occasion in October 1937, Mr Packwood, the soft furnishing buyer, went on an extensive tour of Holland and Germany to procure inexpensive items in readiness to enter the 'Buyer's Gift Week' competition.

Another 'downside' in the previous decade. Kennards first fire in 70 years. A WWI Dennis Fire Engine is on the scene, 1923.

The store also had its down side and suffered with waste and spoils and natural disasters throughout its lifetime. In 1937, which proved to be the worst year's trading in the store's history, a London Bus strike and a local typhoid outbreak occurred. But Kennards, ever resourceful, fought back and gave out a free one month insurance cover to regain customers confidence.

"War on waste" was another constant battle fought within the store. Mr William Kennard founded his success on the "elimination of waste" through hard work and thrift. Mr Driscoll instilled in his employees that "waste was the culprit" with the spoiling of expensive show-cards and window bills, lost articles and so on. The Foreign Fancy department lost "14 statuettes in the nude, five brass tables, one ebony elephant, six Chinese bells and one brass Buddha" to name only a few of supposedly 'borrowed' articles. "No doubt doing duty somewhere to further enhance the beauty of the store" the management stated.

Difficult times do not deter Kennards as this advertisement shows, 1937.

Reproduced by kind permission of the Croydon Advertiser Group.

Also behind the scenes during this time Mr Driscoll's son, Roy, spent a year in department stores in Berlin and Vienna to study window display methods, which were famed for originality and lavishness. In Berlin expensive fittings which cost £250 equipped one window for only three days before the display was scrapped. Thoroughness and amazing passion for detail led the display men to use a yellow colour scheme throughout the store in its "coat week". Unfortunately someone discovered all the coat hangers were of the wrong colour. Hardly an inch of hanger would have shown under the coats but it was vital to re-paint them. It took five men three days to paint 7,000 coat hangers!

In February 1938 " Mlle Veronica, the World's Highest Kicker and Super Dancer" (a pupil of the late Pavlova) was invited to the store to open the 'Ballito' stand where she demonstrated various ranges of stockings. She appeared in the restaurant at 4 pm daily for a week and demonstrated her famous high kick and also opened the new Heala Ray Health Centre.

The annual sales contests were of a week's duration and there was always great rivalry between the household and fashion departments. In May 1938 Mr Newman and Mr Grantham, who were captains of the household and fashion teams, were allotted spending money, window space and advertising allocation. The winners were the household team, with 500 assistants within that department each receiving a cash prize.

Another interesting feature in this period (and now evident in most supermarkets and other places of purchase) was "customers purchasing a pair of 'Air Step' shoes at the advertised price can purchase a second pair at half price".

The store displayed 'mystery tables' in the various household departments, which were linked with microphones connected to loudspeakers fitted throughout the store. Clues were issued over the speakers to guide the customers to the correct sales table. There were also 'tally-ho' bargains. Customers were drawn from department to department by a huntsman's horn, blown by the 'whip of the hunt'!

Charlie Kunz piano music was played all day long over the store's public address system, interrupted by announcements, which began with "Kennards calling, Kennards calling", to draw customers' attention to the various departments,

comically addressed 'Better Baggage' and 'Lids for Kids' (Children's hats)!

In the same decade one could enjoy shopping during the "Four big clock days". The store's clock bell rang at 10 am each morning to commence sales. Different sales occurred in different departments at different hours and the bell would ring to start and finish each sale.

The Clock Sales attracted so many customers that it was necessary for the staff to work from, and on, one end of the counter to the other to serve them, c. mid-1930s.

An alarming experience occurred in mid 1930s on the first morning of one of Kennards' summer sales. The in-house Gazette reported that "about 50 of the 300 or so bargain hunters around the store's windows at opening time had set their hearts on a most beautiful cushion marked at a most ridiculous price". Mr Bristow, the display manager, had been present when the cushion had been snapped up by a happy customer and in front of a very disappointed lady who aimed an all-too-painful punch on his nose! He retained his dignity however and

An artistic duster display, c. mid-1930s.

Above: One of many of the store's promotions, c. mid-1930s.
Below: Customers and this little chap seem quite happy with the 'shopping spree' c. mid-1930s.

was highly commended for his 'inaction' under such very trying circumstances. The Gazette went on to say "We understand that Mr Pumphrey, not to be outdone, is hopefully expecting to have his neck broken during Blue Pencil Week, commencing August 14th"!

The Blue Cross sales we see today most likely originated from Kennards' Blue Pencil Week. This was a biannual event advertised as early as 1939 and it was a common sight to see Mr Driscoll march around the store at the head of a column of shoppers with a blue pencil in his hand and slash prices on the sales tickets along the way. On one occasion he was reprimanded after his court appearance at the local magistrates. 'Jimmy' (as he was known in the trade) Driscoll had been 'carted off' to the police station after his sales promotion brought North End to a halt. He had borrowed two elephants from Bertram Mills Circus to promote the 'Jumbo' birthday sales but the elephants obstructed the whole of North End! (In past times he gave out scrolls to customers giving them "freedom of the store" offering merchandise worth 28 shillings for gold sovereigns (20 shillings). There were printed cartoons in the local press, which depicted his buyer's either groaning or exhilarated at some foolhardy event which was about to take place in the store. Mr Driscoll also gave "Tours of the main cash desk". Many of his ideas were thought up whilst he drove around in his l936 two-seater supercharged 'Auborn' car.

Top left: R. A. Driscoll steps out from a 1914 Hudson vehicle, c. mid-1930s.

Bottom left: Leslie Ford-Thrussell sits astride one of Mr. Bell's (pictured right) ponies in Frith Road to advertise the Blue Pencil Week, c. late 1940s.
Reproduced by kind permission of the Croydon Advertiser Group

Jack Warner, a favourite radio star of the day, made a personal appearance on the last day of the Blue Pencil sales in February 1940 to promote sales. In 1948 Kennards found its porter's boy, Leslie Ford-Thrussell could assist with the promotion. He stood 4'3" tall, weighed around four stone and was an ideal candidate to help with the sales. Kennards sent him to a Saville Row tailor in London where he was fitted out with a pure silk jockey outfit. Dressed in this attire he was seated on one of the Shetland ponies and led around the store by the pony's owner Mr Bell. Accompanied by many children Leslie travelled up and down Frith Road, through the arcade, around the whole of the store including the lifts and held a signpost that read: "FOLLOW THE JOCKEY FOR THE WINNING POST BARGAINS".

There were numerous techniques used in the art of selling and buying. Kennards reported in its Gazette that the late 'Houdini' used to say to himself "What would the public like to see me do?". He found out what his customers wanted and then bent all his energies towards providing it. Kennards applied this method and it proved very successful in its day.

"Where Goods Cost Less Than They Should" was a popular Kennard 'slogan'. Price List of 1966.

Reproduced by kind permission of the Croydon Advertiser Group

Celebrities and Entertainment

British actress Fay Compton opens Kennards' 4th floor extension, 1928.

Kennards' story would be incomplete if one did not mention the many celebrities who came to the store, not just from all parts of Great Britain but from all over the world.

Mr Driscoll firmly believed that, rather than to advertise the store's special departments, the best policy was to advertise store events, to continually draw the public in with "something different". However, the "tongues of the alarmists clanged and clattered. The business was being ruined; the best people would never come in the place", it was reported in its Gazette in 1936. "We're here to sell things; we're not a variety theatre". Then it came to light that whenever a good attraction was put on

sales generally went up. "Just fancy, Billy Bimbo, the Booming Baboon, was actually the means of selling more gloves, more dress materials, more hats, more towels". So along with the attractions came regular events such as Factory Sales, Buyer's Gift Week, Birthday Week, Bands, Exhibitions and a host of other attractions. This was to be characteristic of Kennards in the decades to come.

The earliest photographic record of visiting artistes to the store was in 1928 when Fay Compton, a British actress, opened the new 4th floor extension. Records reveal nothing more until around 1931 when several 'small' screen stars visited the store on different occasions.

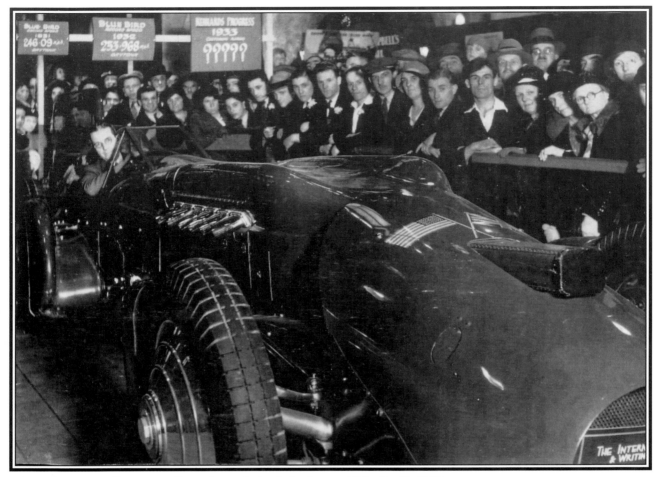

Above: Mr. Driscoll sits proudly in the cockpit of the famous "Bluebird", 1932.
Below: Another view of Sir Malcolm Campbell's "Bluebird" in the store, 1932.

There were exhibitions on two separate occasions of Sir Malcolm Campbell's 'Bluebird'. He set the land speed record at 272.46 mph in February l933 and in September 1935 the same car, after extensive reconstruction, raised the record to 301.13 mph. Kennards claimed to be the first to show the car upon its return to England and with the exception of 'Blue Bird' No. 1 engine it had never before been shown to the public. A small admission charge was made to view the car, the proceeds going to the Croydon General Hospital.

When the car was removed from the store's showroom after the exhibition the workmen, who struggled for many hours, discovered that they need not have "puffed and blown about" if they had only thought to drain from the radiators four hundred weight of water (200 kilogrammes)!

Scenic decorations were prepared by Kennards' artists who were constantly employed making anything from the Blue Pencil signs to paper mache Tudor roses, or back drops and realistic scenery for its visiting guests. The celebrities were greeted by the Management, which usually included Mr Grantham, Mr Harding and the store hostess Mrs Price, along with Mr Driscoll, who would await the celebrity at the top of the grand staircase.

Other attractions in 1935/6 included The Great Omi, the tattooed wonder and 'To-Ya and his Ice Family'; a family of pure Albinos never before seen in England. Kennards had lengthy negotiations to acquire special permission for their entry into this country. They gave half-hourly "mystery and magic" shows in 'The Ice Theatre' on the lower ground floor. Another interest was 'The Ape Man', Mr Castang. He had an extraordinary gift for handling and training apes and of the three apes that entertained the customers, Max, Moritz and Akka, Moritz had been the 'original' for the King Kong film. They performed tricks, which included wire walking, trick cycling and roller-skating.

To-Ya and his "Ice Family", 1935.

There was a replica of an Abyssinian Village where one could see and hear native war dances and songs. 'Hassan's Real Arab Snake Charmers' had a selection of 30 snakes and gave "fascinating demonstrations" to their audience when they released venomous African Cobras, which slithered and hissed on the floor in the Cash & Carry department. Native music, played on flutes, kept the reptiles docile as they swayed to and fro to the hypnotic music. Kennards' representative travelled to Morocco searching for several days by camel before he came across them performing on a street corner. Once again it took lengthy discussions and permission to bring back these 'artistes'.

The Great Omi, the "tattooed wonder". One of many "exhibits" in the store, 1935.

Max and Moritz, c. mid-1930s.

The Abyssinian Village, c. mid-1930s.

Another attraction was 'Hassan and his Indian Troupe'. A special Indian village, with its own 'jungle' was constructed within the store and opened daily to the public who viewed a "baby lion and monkey, streets of carpets and carpet weaving". The 14 Indians on hand sold their Indian arts and crafts and other features included "baffling magicians, a prayer room and a temple of fate".

The Indian Village, c. mid-1930s.

That same year the Croydon Borough Silver Band played every Saturday afternoon in the Provisions Arcade and a special 'musicians gallery' was constructed, which enabled the band to entertain customers without causing obstruction.

In May 1936 'John Lester's Royal Midget Circus' came to Croydon. Although they had appeared at Kennards in 1935, their venue was the Grand Theatre in South Croydon. Whilst in town two of the midgets were married in the local church. The bride and groom were 4 ft tall and their best man, John Lester, was 6 ft 2 ins. His dog, a Great Dane, "accompanied the couple up the aisle and sat quietly in the front pew during the ceremony". The groom was a crooner and singer of cowboy songs with the circus and he was advertised as being the smallest licensed motor car driver in the world. His bride was a dancer and vocalist. Around 3,000 people waited to see the couple exit the church. They had their reception in Kennards' restaurant and the public was invited to the function.

John Lester and the "Midget Bridal Party", 1935.

In August 1936 Kennards erected a fully equipped film studio on the roof of its store. The idea of discovering whether Croydon had any potential 'Garbos or Gables' was a novel and exciting scheme and ran in conjunction with the Croydon Times. The public was invited to send in their photo portraits to the 'Film Editor' at Kennards and for those who had 'possibilities' a screen test followed. A fully qualified producer was engaged by the store's management in the hope of making a film to show at certain local cinemas. British producers and film casting departments were to be shown the film tests, in the hope that those with genuine talent might have an opportunity to reach 'stardom'. The records are not clear but the film business was abandoned.

In October 1937 'Ali Baba' and his troupe of Indian Performers appeared at Kennards. "Magic and miraculous conjuring tricks, a vanishing

Harem and an Indian Basket of Death" were the highlights. Ali Baba also successfully staged escapes from prison stocks, an exact replica of those once used at Newgate Prison and offered a £100 challenge to all comers who could emulate his escape. There was also 'Hassan', the "famous boy performer from the Punjab", who thrilled his audience when the "nautch dancer" demonstrated this centuries old art.

'Ace airwoman' Jean Batten, who was the first person to hold the England-Australia flight record in both directions, was greeted at Croydon airport in October 1937 by around 10,000 people. She later visited Kennards to present their 'Buyer's Gift Week Cup' to one of the fashion buyers. The crowd was "Ten deep along both sides of North End. Strained against a police-cordon outside Kennards", reported the Croydon Times, "with scarcely an inch to spare over the whole ground-floor space of the store. North End looked a little bit like London on Coronation night". North End was so packed with people that buses and trams could not stop outside Kennards and other traffic was near to a standstill. Miss Batten, besieged by autograph hunters in the store, needed escorting by security men to clear the passage and hold back the crowds.

Jean Batten with Mr. Driscoll about to present the Buyer's Cup, 1937.

In 1938 Kennards opened a "Golf school" under the directorship of Kenneth Wilson, author of an unusual golfing book. It was to revolutionise the art of learning the game by the use of a 'bucket and bayonet'! The book created national interest and British Movietone News expressed a great wish to

Claude Dampier (left) watches the bucket and bayonet method of golf, 1938.

film this method of learning golf, so Kennards was pleased to advertise the filming which took place on the store's roof. Who better for the role as a 'pupil' for the event than the stage, screen and radio star, Claude Dampier, a comedian, known as the "professional idiot". The Women's League of Health and Beauty demonstrated the new tech-

The Women's League of Health and Beauty demonstrate the art of the golf swing, 1938.

nique using certain strokes with a bayonet and by swinging a bucket of water to develop the correct swing. This method made Claude Dampier remark: "What are they doing?" He was told this was a new system to learn golf. Upon the reply Claude said: "Oh, I thought they were waiting for the cow to

Kennards' miniature golf course. It was divided into two parts. Six "holes" on the first floor and 12 more "holes" on the roof of the store. The golf course opened for several weeks in 1930.

turn up"! The author struggled to teach his difficult pupil. Claude tried, unsuccessfully, to emulate the girls and sat down with a sigh and said "Wearing plus-fours will always be my nearest approach to becoming a real golfer". The Croydon Times stated: "It is believed that this will be the first time a departmental store has been used by a news film company".

A month later Croydon became the stage for a Royal visit, by Her Majesty Queen Mary. She visited Croydon to present the new colours of the 4th Battalion, the Queen's Royal Regiment, of which she was the Colonel-in-Chief. The ceremony took place in the grounds of Whitgift Middle School. Kennards 'went to town' by putting on numerous in-store attractions, for it also had its own 84th birthday celebrations to cater for. There was a magnificent exhibition of the replicas of the Crown Jewels, complete in its own Tower of London setting, including a Beefeater guard. These Jewels were "replicas of the identical Regalia used

in the Coronation Rehearsal and can only be seen at Kennards". This was staged on the exhibition floor on the ground floor.

C. B. Harrison's Glamour Girls featured at many fashion venues, including Kennards, as seen in this photograph, c. mid-1930s.

Lupino Lane and Teddy St. Denis. Stars in the store, 1938. Reproduced by kind permission of the Croydon Advertiser Group

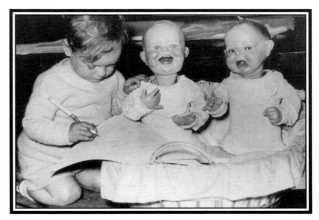

One contented baby awaits the competition results, accompanied by two dolls of mixed feelings! 1937.

Film-land glamour girls fashioned 'Bukta Swim Suits' in the 'Riviera Bathing Parades' which the store held daily during the Royal Gala Week. Lupino Lane and Teddie St Denis, the stars in the musical comedy "Me and My Girl", played at the Victoria Palace Theatre in London presented prizes to the winners of the Baby Show competition, which had over 700 entries.

During the birthday celebrations the whole store took on the appearance of a huge variety theatre. Magnificent decorations, inside and outside the store, gave more than a hint it was about to 'entertain' yet again. Cabaret shows (given by children from local dancing schools) and "Old Folk's Tea Parties" were held in the main restaurant. Kennards' own orchestra and the Van Der Vann's Dutch Gypsy Orchestra were engaged to play from mid-day to 6 pm daily. Birthday bells, with "Carillon birthday tunes" were broadcast in the store every hour. The world famous Dagenham Girl Pipers commenced the celebrations by heading the procession from West Croydon station. They 'piped' a model cake in ceremony through the store, accompanied by Snow White and two of the famous Seven Dwarfs who had travelled from the 'Daily Mail Ideal Home Exhibition'.

The "Big Drummer" parades with the world famous Dagenham Girl Pipers, 1960.

Kennards was reported to be famous for its "attractions and lavish entertainments". The "Mecca of the Stars of Stage, Screen and Radio", c. mid-1930s..

Jack Warner, c. 1940s.

Margaret Lockwood, c. 1940s.

More stars shone in the store. In 1940, Jack Warner, a British actor, known in later years for the "Dixon of Dock Green" television series and Godfrey Winn, author and journalist also appeared. In 1942, Charles Coburn, an American 'character actor' came to the store. In 1945 Richard Murdoch, well known for the radio comedy series "Round the Horn" appeared. Group Captain 'Cats' Eyes Cunningham' and 'Tin Legs' Bader, the famous legless fighter pilot, were other popular guest visitors. The Billy Cotton Band, Tommy Trinder and Prince Monolulu were all visitors on separate occasions. There were also visits from Dukes, Lords and even an Archbishop judging by Kennards press cutting books of the period.

Michael Rennie, who had leading film roles visited the store in 1947 along with Joe Baksi, an American Heavyweight boxer who fought for the World Championship. Margaret Lockwood (a 'local girl' from Upper Norwood) who was a British film actress came in 1948 and on other occasions. Jimmy Hanley, Petula Clark, Katie Boyle, Googie Withers, Norman Wisdom and Dirk Bogarde were all visitors to Kennards in the early 1950s and there were many more. In the 1970s Pat Phoenix, who played 'Elsie Tanner' in the television series 'Coronation Street', opened a new department and was the last of the celebrities to be recorded in Kennards' archives.

Kennards' celebrities numbered up to six or more each year, together with numerous attractions. The store's celebrity calls were a welcome sight and irresistible to a generation which had little entertainment in those pre-television days. So what better place and time to show off some of the stars in its store. Kennards became a social centre and a social success.

Children's Corners

Kennards went to extraordinary lengths to keep customers' children amused for they knew parents' problems were halved if children were catered for. The earliest records of Kennards providing entertainment for "Croydon kiddies" goes back to the late 1920s when the Shetland pony rides were introduced. The Frith Road/Keeley Road corner extension and main (through store) arcade were not yet in existence, but along these roads could be seen two of the original ponies "Nigger and Venus; a common sight disappearing around the corner at a canter". The ponies were initiated by a Mr Bell in 1928 and were stabled in old buildings in a yard off Drummond Road. A Mrs Miller was employed a year later to assist him and her little ponies, Wendy, Linda and Judy gave pleasure to many children. These ponies "worked a rota; one in the mornings; two in the afternoons" and made "two circuits of their track", along a section of the pavement and later on through part of the newly built Frith Road arcade. Several customers stated that the ponies also travelled through the main arcade in bad weather and the weight limit per child was five stone (32 kg). In 1966 Mrs Miller

Kennards' records reveal that "Bunkumsnorus" was "captured Xmas 1922", 1922.

retired. The Frith Road store frontage alteration and re-development in Drummond Road had obliterated the ponies stables and track.

Kennards' zoo animals were housed close to the ponies' stables from July 1930 onwards. They were exhibited in-situ, for it was advertised "Everyone knows where the ponies are; the Zoo will be found further down the same road". Cages contained Rhesus Monkeys, a Sloth Bear caged next to an Arabian Camel (called Clarence), Syrian sheep, Peacocks, Red Deer; a Sacred Cow (a Zebu), and a variety of birds. By November that year more animal attractions were added, namely a lion and lioness named Leo and Florence, Percy the Porcupine, Willie the Wolf and Harry the Hyena. Kennards gave one word of warning though, "We cannot accept responsibility for what may happen if people will poke their fingers through the bars"! The store advertised that it was "the first real Zoo

Mrs. Miller gives young Janet Ardley (seated on 'Linda') and Vernon Etridge (on 'Judy') the last of Kennards' pony rides, 1966.
Reproduced by kind permission of the Croydon Advertiser Group

Above: Some of the animals from the "real zoo". Kennards made alternative arrangements for their winter quarters, c. mid-1930s. Below left: The cheetahs were "temporary exhibits" in the store, c. mid-1930s.

ever to be seen in Croydon" but with the outbreak of the Second World War this 'real Zoo' ceased.

Railway rides were available on a miniature passenger steam locomotive on the store's roof and was another treat for children and adults alike. This train also doubled as Father Christmas's Dreamland Express.

Railway rides enjoyed in "the playground in the sky" on Kennards' roof, c. mid-1930s.

Young Master Robin Kennard about to enjoy a ride on the steam locomotive on the store's roof, with his father William Dudley Kennard (left) and grandfather "Mr. William", c. late 1930s.
Reproduced by kind permission of the Croydon Advertiser Group

The most outstanding of the children's activities was undoubtedly the 'Croydon Times Bunny Club'. Kennards' Gazette of June 1935 states of the club's existence from 1932, which was claimed to be the largest and most popular club run by a weekly newspaper. Mrs Hatch, a director of the Croydon Times, formed the children's club and, within a month of its running, membership had reached 4,000. This was not solely run as an ordinary newspaper club, or weekly children's feature, but actually reached out to its members by its "live entertainment" factor. Mrs Hatch approached Kennards for support as a social venue and the store became "an organisation equally alive to the possibilities and pleasures of entertaining".

In August 1932 children's parties were arranged in Kennards' new Cash and Carry store extension and on each of a five-day period "700 Bunnies had a splendid tea provided for them", followed by fancy dress parades through the store and onto the roof. The same year the Bunnies attended a Midget Circus at Kennards' open-air performances in Park Hill Recreation Ground. Over the years the club also held numerous concert parties. Amusing monologues, serious ballad to music hall songs and dancing, anything from tap to can-can was staged. Whistling solos and Dickens recitations were other performances given at these concerts. They also held fetes and sports and social functions to raise funds for local charities and radio broadcasts were made on several occasions on BBC 'London Regional' programme 'Children's Hour'. The club received congratulatory letters from all corners of the country on their charity fund raising.

Mrs Hatch also brought to the children a real "flesh and blood uncle, that genial figure Uncle

The Author's cousin, Miriam Garcia (bottom row, centre, marked X) was one of the youngest Bunny Club members, 1937. Reproduced by kind permission of the Croydon Advertiser Group

Enjoying one of the many entertainments on Kennards' roof, c. late 1930s.

Tom". He was the club's producer and although his real identity remained a secret he was always present at the children's functions and became an outstanding personality in Croydon. Regular visits to the Davis Theatre in Croydon were organised, where as many as 4,000 children were entertained. These were "happy, excited children, cheering wildly at the sight of Uncle Tom" and singing not only their own Bunny Club song but also all the popular songs of the day. By 1937 membership had passed the 24.000 mark.

Spectacular views and entertainment were also provided and enjoyed in "Croydon's new playground up in the sky". By 1935 Kennards' new Keely Road/Frith Road extension and main arcade were near to completion and afforded generous roof top space for numerous events from August that year. This new roof expanse consisted of a 'garden',

a full size tennis court and a sports arena, together with a 220 yard (200 metre) track around the roof top circumference. A new roof top restaurant was opened and bookings for all these amenities were made available to schools and other sectors of the community. Open-air bands and 'sea-side' concerts were regular attractions held on Saturday afternoons. The store held its first 'novel dog show' (a mid-week, three-day event) that same year. Kennards did not want a "highbrow affair", with entry names such as "Prince Petulengro of Purley Park", or "Puce Percival the third of Pump Pail", so they invented classes for "the quaintest dog; the most intelligent dog" and a competition for "the dog with the sweetest expression". They even had a "begging competition, in which some very conscientious dogs, knowing the local bye-laws refused to take part"!

Baby competitions, dog shows and a host of attractions enjoyed in Kennards' "playground in the sky", c. mid-1930s.

The 'Monkey Village' paid a second visit to Kennards in 1936 and had a complete colony of performing monkeys (50 in total) who amused their audience with tricks, riding model trains, aeroplanes and motor cars. But the monkeys weren't always so friendly. 'Joss', a baboon on exhibition, escaped from his cage and evaded capture for an hour. He ran through the toy department, up a flight of stairs and reached the roof via the café. He "enjoyed himself immensely and to the delight of the crowds watching him in North End he danced". His keeper tried in vain to tempt him down with bananas, biscuits and even a looking glass. Joss became very interested however in Kennards' cameraman and "posed nicely while his photograph was taken". His curiosity however was his undoing. He came too close to the photographer and was caught. The Croydon Times reported: "Shortly after his capture another monkey who had been brought out to try to snare Joss undid his leash and ran onto a flag pole. He was caught however, without any fuss", but back in his cage Joss was "in a very bad temper and tore up the floorboards. He had to be removed to a smaller cage in the basement".

The store held annual children's fancy dress and Christmas parties and catered for over 400 children. Entertainment was given by Dorothea Marno's Orchestra and 'Cardi the conjurer' who performed startling tricks. Pupils of 'Margery

"Escape bid" by Joss the baboon, 1936.

Reproduced by kind permission of the Croydon Advertiser Group

One of the children's Fancy Dress Parties in Kennards. Mr. Harding's son, Bernard, sits in the front row in his "sailor suit", 1935.

Moore's School of Dancing' performed Cinderella. The "little guests" received "bon-bons, balloons and novelties" and although the party continued for over an hour "the children just wouldn't go home".

By 1937 children could see colour films during the school holidays in Kennards' 300 seating 'cottage theatre' decorated in colours of gold, silver and old rose. This was situated on the first floor and was also used for the store's variety programmes. The 'Children's Outfitter' stated that the theatre was "believed to be the first in England to show colour films". The Toy Bazaar displayed full size working models of nursery rhyme characters and there were roundabouts of miniature flying boats and planes, which were a great attraction.

A favourite in 1938 was the Easter Egg Farm, situated in the children's department and set in a backdrop of an old-world farmstead. Hundreds of live baby chicks were added to its scenery to make it more realistic. There was also a small pet's zoo in the main arcade, which was a recognisable feature in the 1950s and 1960s and provided yet another magnet for the children.

There is no doubt that one of the store's slogans: "we entertain to sell and we sell to entertain" had true meaning.

Children's amusements – an aeroplane roundabout, c. mid-1930s.

Top left: Real "baby" chicks back in 1923.

Top right: Chocolate Easter Eggs for sale at the "farm house", 1938.

Bottom: Kennards' "scenic artists" made a realistic backdrop for the farm, 1938.

Christmas at Kennards

Not only did the children delight in the store's seasonal festivities over the decades, but so too did the adults, judging by the photographs! The Croydon Times devoted a whole page to Kennards' Christmas entertainment throughout November and December each year. Kennards claimed to be the "largest individual contributor of rates; the largest individual consumer of electricity and the biggest advertisers in the Borough".

In the 1930s Kennards had a "Special Children's Shopping Week". Sales assistants were made available as "aunties" and "uncles"; three of each, on three floor levels in the store, to assist the children to choose presents. If there was money to spare after buying presents then the remainder could be spent on a pony or train ride, or a visit to the children's café upstairs to buy "a special cup of real tea, bread and butter and special little cakes".

Opposite: North End packed with pedestrians on Father Christmas's arrival, c. mid-1930s.
Above: Portland Road railway bridge South Norwood, looking north, c. 1940s..

Father Christmas made his appearances at Kennards in various modes of transport throughout the decades. He made grand entrances on the store's locomotive, the 'Dreamland Express', through the new main arcade to his house on the lower ground floor where Mother Christmas would also make an appearance. One year his travel arrangements were via Thornton Heath, where he was met by the band of the Dagenham Girl pipers and travelled through Broad Green, West Croydon and along North End where hundreds of children and adults lined the route to greet him. A van equipped with a loudspeaker, announcing Father Christmas's arrival, playing lively music, along with a string of humorous anecdotes, completed the procession. Crowds of children gathered outside and inside the store. Father and Mother Christmas were greeted by Mr Harding (Director and General Manager) and shown their "cosy little home, which they will occupy until Christmas". Another treat for the children, at a small charge, was to partake in "breakfast, dinner or tea with Father Christmas" in the restaurant.

Above: Crowds outside Kennards' mammoth store, c. mid-1930s.
Left: Reported to be "the largest Father Christmas in the world". He weighted 43 stone with a girth of 6'8" (2m) round the waist, 1943.

In 1931 Father Christmas arrived in his 'treasure ship' and opened Kennards' Bazaar door with a huge golden key to enter his 'grotto'. The Christmas scene during the Second World War depicted the trenches, where he greeted the children from his 'war-time dugout' headquarters. He also arrived by horse and wagon and even a helicopter in later years, changing in size and height over the decades.

Other Christmas attractions included 'Leon Volpre's' indoor circus, which gave shows several times daily in 1936. Six dogs and Shetland ponies did 'turns' in one of their acts. The animals also took part in mock court martial scenes and an accident scene in which a tiny King Charles Spaniel played the part of a nurse. Children saw a 20-minute show of the Marionettes theatre, where 'Bilton's Minimites' gave hourly shows. The dolls "in quaint costumes" acted out the stories of Aladdin, Cinderella and Dick Whittington.

Left: One of John Lester's midgets portrays Father Christmas whilst sat on Mr. Bell's pony, at Croydon General Hospital, c. mid-1930s. Right: Bilton's Marionettes, 1936.

In December 1937 Dr Ford, the flea trainer, returned to Kennards with his "Juggling Chinese Flea Circus". Kennards advertised that "over 5,000 people a week visited the show". The performing fleas pulled miniature chariots that were 800 times their own weight. Dr Ford informed the public that it took three weeks to train a flea to perform. He also challenged anyone to prove his fleas were not alive or the performances not genuine, offering a £100 cheque to the contrary.

In the same year American-Indians Chief Blue Sky and Indian Brave Young Calf came over from the sun-scorched prairies of Manitoba. 'Chief Blue Sky and his band of Indian Braves and Squaws' had appeared in the famous American film "The Last of the Mohicans". They gave live perform-

Father Christmas arrives in an early 1920 Austin car accompanied by "Chief Blue Sky's Braves", 1937.

ances of their native songs, dances and tomahawk displays in the store, along with reproductions of native wedding ceremonies and other rituals. Little Calf and one of the 'squaws', Princess Moira, lodged with my Uncle, Jack Garcia, in his house in Church Path, Croydon. Jack, a Surrey Street market trader who had once 'trodden the boards' appeared in the Wild West shows as a 'Zorro' type figure. These shows continued for many weeks leading up to Christmas.

The Croydon Times stated that Kennards' customers could "walk through four miles of store to procure everything you want for Christmas".

Top left: Princess Moira with some of the Braves in the store, 1937.

Top right: The author's Uncle, Jack Garcia, was a "Zorro" type cowboy in the Wild West Shows, 1937.

Bottom left: Dean Hilbourne, aged three years, with his Christmas present at Kennards, 1946.

Left: A Wild West Show staged in Kennards Store back in 1932.
Reproduced by kind permission of the Croydon Advertiser Group

Right: Numerous Christmas attractions advertised in 1937.
Reproduced by kind permission of the Croydon Advertiser Group

Below: Christmas treats "in-store" in Kennards, North End, 1960.

Kennards in Wartime

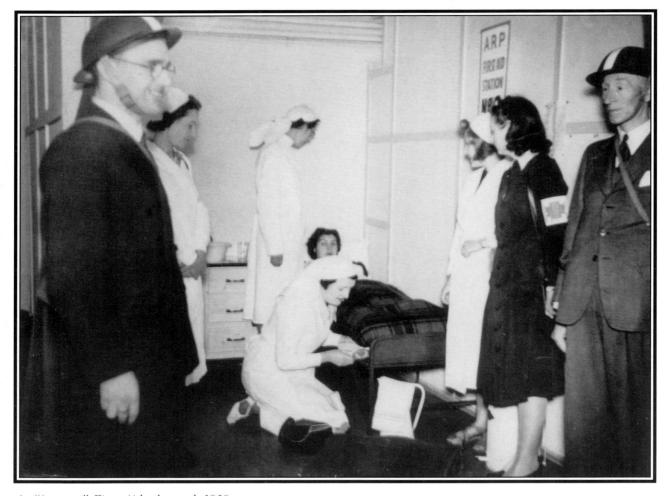

An "in-store" First Aid rehearsal, 1939.

"Fifty thousand of the Croydon public and 18,000 children and parents evacuated from Croydon", exclaimed Kennards during the Second World War. The management was concerned. There were fewer customers, stock control and despatch problems, staff considerations and the 'black-out' to contend with. It survived the air raids and also did its own raiding by buying the entire stock of a large West End store, Thompson's of Tottenham Court Road. The stock, valued at £15,000, was purchased for £8,000.

Furniture, linens, dress materials, West End gowns, china, coats and more were bought for wartime sales.

Customers need not be alarmed when shopping in the store during an air raid. Each assistant took his or her customer down to the shelters in the basement where there was "a wonderful new air raid shelter, built to Home Office specifications for 800 persons". This was advertised as being "decorated and comfortably equipped with an underground hairdressing section", which enabled customers "to be attended during the period of an air raid alarm"! There were two fully-equipped First Aid Stations, controlled by an ex-officer of the Royal Army Medical Corp and assisted by over 100 of Kennards' internal ARPs (air raid pre-caution) staff trained 18 months previously by Mr Cawte of the carpet department.

Many ARP requirements were sold in the store. These included blankets, sheets for billeting, black-out papers, special light shades, first aid equipment for home and industry and gas mask containers. Mr Driscoll, ever resourceful, beat the blackout and lighting regulations by using a quantity of luminous paint which he "splashed around his dimly lit premises and proclaimed them to be the brightest spot in Croydon".

Mr Porter, the furniture buyer, had been busy in Birmingham and completed a "big deal". Mr Nichols the merchandise manager had travelled to The Midlands searching for bargains in blanket and household goods and "hourly reports" had been received by the store from the underwear and hosiery buyers in Leicester. Kennards stated that: "Air raid or no air raid we shall open as usual".

Forty-three members of staff were serving in His Majesty's Forces and the 'Kennards' Comfort Club', formed by the staff, sent parcels of various articles for colleagues in the forces. 'Kennards' Knitting Circle' also gave hand knitted cardigans, scarves, mittens, socks and more, made by Miss Manley and her band of helpers.

Kennards had its own 'Staff Fire Squad' trained by the Croydon Fire Brigade. Training exercises were held on the store's roof, led by their officer, Mr Beretta, of the sports department. Thirty fully-trained members of staff became experienced in dealing with peace and wartime fire-fighting tech-niques designed for a modern store. Uniforms, equipment and lectures were provided. Full dress rehearsals were also staged during the first week of the war and continued until the war ended.

A special duplicated alarm system in the store meant it was possible to have at least ten men with three pumps and 60 gallons of water at any given point on the premises within two minutes, inclu-ding the workshops and outbuildings. A 3,000 gallon emergency canvas tank of water was situated on the store's roof in case of damage to the water main. Displays, given before the store's Directors and Executives showed how to extinguish

Members of the "Staff Fire Squad" on Kennards' roof, 1939.

Another rehearsal. An incendiary bomb is released in the store, c. early 1940s.

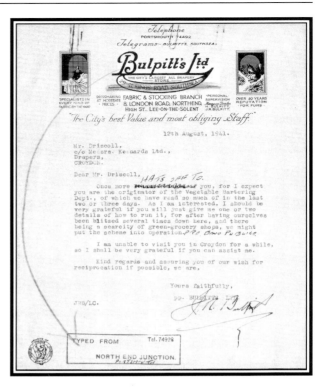

A congratulatory letter from Bulpitts, 1941.

incendiary bombs and the great skills developed by the store's fire-fighting teams were to prove crucial during the war. Kennards was saved from batches of 30 incendiary bombs that fell across its roof during air raids.

For a short period in late 1939 Kennards assisted the Ministry of Health when they opened a blood transfusion enrolling centre in its store. On the first Saturday nearly 2,000 donors were "tested and registered".

In 1941 an age-old barter system was held in Kennards' car park. This market was termed "The Housewives' Dream". Alleged to be the "first market of its kind in the country", stated the Croydon Times. Local allotment holders, like many other people, cultivated allotments and back gardens so had a wealth of the vegetable kingdom around them. For a short period of time a surplus of vegetables was available. The exchange of vegetables for clothing coupons was a successful scheme. Vouchers to the value of the produce were given which could be spent in the store. Shoes, blankets, furniture and other goods could also be acquired.

The Ministry of Food followed this 'experiment' with interest as they encouraged people to "dig for victory" and grow produce. Kennards stated that it ran this market at a loss to try to help with fair food distribution. A portion of the car park was allocated to the Surrey gardeners and allotment holders to set up special stalls to sell their produce. Within the space of a few minutes on the first day of opening 300 shoppers bought all the vegetables on sale. Although of short duration this venture was recorded overseas in The New York Sun and the Daily Herald in New Zealand.

Kennards helped with the war effort in many ways. It was very public-spirited and held several 'Battle for Fuel' exhibitions during 1942 and early 1943. Conserving electricity, water, coal and gas by individual consumers was of prime concern to the country when national need was great. Savings helped to "feed the guns and keep the bombers flying, along with fuel to speed munitions". In November 1942 the exhibition was visited by nearly 300,000 people in three weeks. Visitors viewed wartime cooking demonstrations given by the Ministry

This air view of Kennards' store shows where the thirty incendiary bombs were dropped, c. early 1940s.

Above: The Mayor of Croydon, Alderman Harding (left) tours the Battle for Fuel Exhibition, with Town Clerk, Ernest Taberner, 1942.
Right: A recruiting stand in Kennards' main arcade, 1939.

"Gert and Daisy" with Mr. Driscoll (centre) and exhibition officials. Their humour livened the Battle for Fuel Exhibitions. 1942.

of Food. Exhibits included a gun turret of a bomber, the inside workings of a tank and aircraft bomb racks. Many photographs, displays, films and lectures and an 'Information Bureau', all staffed by experts from the various services, demonstrated how fuel savings could be achieved by the average household. Well-known personalities spoke every day at the exhibition and Elsie and Doris Waters (Gert and Daisy) made their appearance giving a "homely, humorous form of address, punctuated by typical wise cracks and back-chat for which their stage performances were renowned".

Government 'Holidays at Home' programmes held at Municipal Borough level was designed to reduce demand for travel. Stores like Kennards participated by providing entertainment. Kennards' attractions within and on the store's roof took

place in June 1943 when local children were invited to a 'Sports Carnival Week'. Events, which were open to registered youth organisations, included egg and spoon races, balloon blowing, running, skipping and three-legged races. Boxing, juvenile athletics and fancy dress parades were also incorporated. There was a competition for the best decorated bicycle, pram and sugar boxes (handcarts). Professor Niblo appeared with his bird circus. It was claimed to be "the only show of its kind in the world". His birds were "trained to fire anti-aircraft guns and draw tanks"! These activities helped fund the Croydon salvage drive.

More roof-top entertainment occurred when Kennards held the 'South of England Red Cross Open Rabbit Show', which was officially opened by His Grace The Duke of Norfolk. Over 200 top

One of the "Holidays at Home" programmes designed for the children, c. early 1940s.

A steady hand is needed for the painting of seams, c. early 1940s.

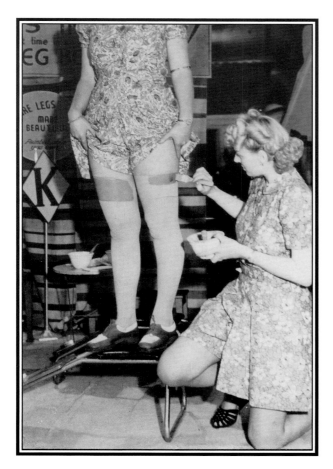

Kennards were one of the first stores to introduce the painting of stockings on bare legs, c. early 1940s.

breed classes as well as the domestic rabbit club (4,000 entries) took part, judged by over 20 of England's best known judges, with the profits (from entry and admission charges) going to the Red Cross. Further events included the East Yorkshire Regiment who gave free concerts in a two-day event in the main restaurant and ground floor fashion department, with donations given to the Prisoners of War Fund.

In 1947 a very similar set up to that of the barter system of 1941 'The Housewives' Dream' was once again operating in Kennards' car park and arcade. This was a 'grower to buyer' market and was established because there was a glut of produce in Britain. The hot summer that year brought forward the ripening of fruit and vegetables in great quantities. Foreign produce also flooded the market place and traders in the wholesale markets, such as Covent Garden, witnessed lorries departing with

The "Grower Vegetable Market" in Kennards' car park, 1947.

"Two thousand housewives jammed the Croydon arcade", stated the National newspapers. Prices were fixed on the spot. "How much for turnips?" asked the grower. The crowd of customers roared "2d" and they were promptly sold for 2d. Lettuce sold for 3d and 4d each (shop price was 10d). Plums sold for 4d a pound when the shop price was double. Local greengrocers and the Surrey Street market traders complained about unfair competition. So incensed were the stall-holders that ten of them went to the arcade to criticise the grower's association. Just prior to their arrival the housewives had been giving their views to the BBC recording unit. "Who's been overcharging us for years?" the housewives demanded. "We'll show you what we think of you". And they did. Broadcasting forgotten, the angry housewives, more than 100 of them, waved their shopping bags and mobbed the Surrey Street traders who were "jostled and

Another happy customer, c. late 1940s.

unsold vegetables destined for destruction as they returned to the farms to be ploughed back into the land or made into animal feed.

A dozen Sussex growers led by Mr John Addison of East Grinstead, Sussex took action and formed a "farm to public trading association" designed to sell direct to the general public in revolt against the wholesale markets which had maintained high prices when there was a surplus. Kennards gave the farmers the use of the arcade rent-free. As shop prices stayed high the farmers kept theirs low. The move and mood to fight the "600% middlemen profiteers" was strong and continued. The market gardeners defied the Ministry of Food orders and continued to trade. The Ministry officials finally sanctioned the farm to public trading after they visited the store and learnt that the growers had licences to sell their own produce and were fully entitled to trade in the arcade.

roundly abused and engulfed by the surging crowd of hostile women and hustled out of the arcade entrance"!

So this was yet another successful scheme for Kennards which made a huge impact, not only locally but world wide too. On the first day of trading the early morning queue totalled over 500. Two thousand, five hundred customers were served by mid-day, which brought over 100 newspaper and press photographers to the store along with three World Press News Agencies. The arcade was filmed and nationwide newsreels made by Movietone, Pathe Gazette, Paramount and J. Arthur Rank. The BBC broadcast the events in their news bulletins and included a feature programme. Films were distributed overseas. After eight days the grower's market still made headline news in all the national newspapers.

It looks as though another housewives' dream has come true, as customers await their bundles (4 prs) of stockings, c. late 1940s.

The Mock Tudor Arcade

One of the original pet shops in the main arcade, 1937.

"When a business man dares to do something new and different – when he does his best to run his business at full speed – he makes it safer. In a word, the man who is afraid to take any risk is running the greatest risk of all – the risk of bankruptcy. Everyone knows that Kennards fly high and fast. It is entirely due to the Management's flare for doing something 'new and different', not just once, but constantly. And just as this running at full speed makes the business safer, so does it make things safer for each of us, if we do our bit and do it well." The statement came from the management in their in-house Gazette and there was proof enough they were prepared to take huge risks, for they dreamt up yet another idea and opened a 'street of shops'. This venture, which operated within the main arcade from 1937, was so successful that it is still remembered with fondness by Croydonians and customers to this present day.

By the early 1950s the arcade had changed in style into an 'Elizabethan Walk', with around a dozen small lockable individual mock Tudor style shops. These were rented out to the 'Arcadians', individual traders who operated their own private businesses. Trades such as a tailor and stocking repair shop, ice cream and candy floss shops, together with a photographer's and a watch repair shop, an estate agency and an aquarium. There was also a small zoo and a small pet shop, which traded in close harmony.

Have you seen Kennard's

Elizabethan
Tudor Walk?

With it's old style

Bun Shoppe.   Aquarium,
Tailor and   Pet and Bird Shops,
Watchmaster.   and Zoo
among other attractions.

The reverse side of a cash till receipt depicting the Tudor arcade, c. 1950s.

The Shetland ponies continued their rounds along the Frith Road frontage. Just inside the main arcade, on the left-hand side, was a department that housed the toys and Christmas fairs each year. There was also a merry go round here (near to the Frith Road/Keeley Road entrance). It had real ponies, around six in number, harnessed to a colourful carousel. On the right hand side of the arcade (from the Frith Road entrance) was an aquarium. This was a feature from the previous decade or two and a Mrs. Riley ran the shop. Although it looked large from its exterior, the shop had little depth and was dimly lit and devoid of natural light. On display were many small size tanks containing tropical fish and another larger tank, which housed around three alligators. The fish were for sale but the alligators, which measured about 4 ft in length, were used purely as exhibits. It was a common sight to see Mrs. Riley taking an alligator out of the tank, lay it over her shoulder and stroke its back whilst talking to a customer. When a customer needed serving the alligator was replaced in its tank!

At the top (North End) end of the arcade there was an oriental stall, which sold all kinds of mystic eastern potions; the air full of aromas from the joss sticks which were constantly burned. The salesman had a long dangling moustache and thought to be a genuine Chinese mandarin until a customer heard him shout out one day in a Cockney accent "Don't put the baby on the table Madam, it's solid oak!".

Many customers recall seeing small caged animals within the main arcade, but they were also exhibited upon the 'bridge' or wide gallery in past times. This bridge spanned the width of the arcade a little way up the sloping Elizabethan street and was approached by steps, which also gave access to the first floor departments. Real life working models of nursery rhyme figures, such as 'Old King Cole' and 'Little Miss Muffet' were also found here. There were penny slot machines where one paid to view different 'scenes' of miniature working models such as an Egyptian mummy emerging from his tomb, or a drunk spooked by a spectre in a church graveyard. Such machines were the vogue in fun fairs and seaside amusement arcades. There was also an ornate clock, which displayed miniature elfin figures, each holding a bell that played a tune when rung on the hour.

There were "parrots that chattered with astonishing rapidity and clarity and friendly monkeys" to name only a few inhabitants, which increased the store's pet food sales. Customers recalled the "constant screeching of the monkeys and strong odours permeating the arcade, with the smell of the ponies and zoo which met you at the North End entrance".

John & Rosa Wood's trade (the first 'Arcadians' in the Tudor walk in the early 1950s) was that of watchmaker and repairer. They sold watchbands, jewellery, necklace chains, ear-rings and gave an ear-piercing service. Mrs. Wood carried out the ear piercing 'operations' and any customer who wanted their ears pierced and was of a nervous disposition was offered a 'tot of brandy' beforehand, just to calm their nerves. Mr. Wood carried out the jewellery, watch and clock repairs and re-strung pearl necklaces. On one occasion John Wood was busy doing a watch repair, with his head bent low over the job in hand, when a voice said "Hello, hello". He thought this was a customer and enquired to what the person wanted. The voice said again "Hello, hello". Mr. Wood directed his wife to see to the impatient person, but his wife informed him that there was no customer to be seen. Upon looking up Mr. Wood saw a parrot strutting around on the arcade walkway. It had fluttered down from the bridge situated above their shop.

Above: One of two shops rented by Mr. Wood the watch repairer, . c. early 1950s.
Below: Mr. Wood, with pipe in mouth, in his mock Tudor shop, c. early 1950s.

In 1951 Kennards celebrated its 100th birthday. (Confusion as to whether Kennards was established in 1851, 1852, 1853 or 1854 has always presented itself – even to them! See chapter one for details). A realistic replica of Kennards' original double fronted shop was erected in the main arcade and a 'transport exhibition', displaying penny-farthing cycles and old time motor cars was also on show

here. "Films through the Ages" was another attraction and Googie Withers, "Britain's famous film star" officially opened the centenary birthday celebrations.

By mid to late 1960s the travel bureau, which had operated in the main store, rented space in the arcade. Mrs. Leach, who joined the store in 1949,

A "Travel" section in Kennards' store, 1960.

ran the agency. The Bureau started out as a coach and theatre booking agency only and offered trips for the Royal Tournament, theatre shows up London and so on, but then branched out and advertised local holidays to Eastbourne, Hastings and St. Leonard's on Sea in Sussex. The travel holidays bookings grew as travelling extended and they gave a wider choice of holidays to Europe, America and Canada. Their business was mostly carried out by letter writing in the early part of their operation and very little was organised or booked on the telephone. Mrs. Leach organised annual two-week exhibitions each January and Kennards allowed the agency 'advertising space' within the store where it occupied a whole department floor to generate more business.

The main arcade (Hedgis Yard) was officially closed in 1979. It meant the demise of the Mock Tudor arcade and all its attractions. Although they now belong to a distant past, customer's present recollections are not dimmed.

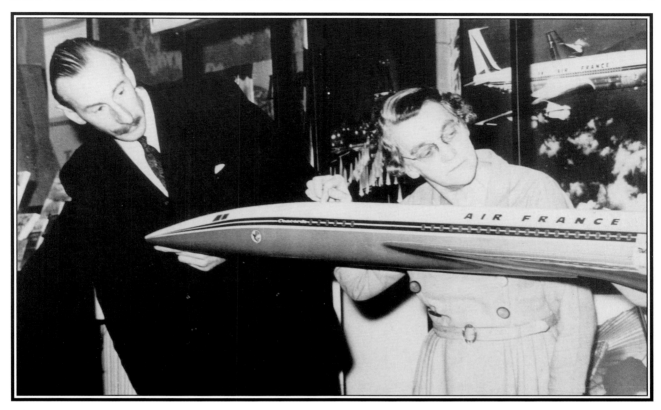

Above: Mrs. Leach with Mr. Hodgson the Advertising Manager at the travel exhibition in Kennards. A sign on the Concorde model reads "Do not Touch"! 1965. Reproduced by kind permission of the Croydon Advertiser Group
Below: David Cox at the top of the main arcade with his shoe repair business, 1978.

Debenhams' Debut

Debenhams came to prominence when 21 year old William Debenham, the son of a Suffolk farmer, bought an equal partnership with a Thomas Clark in 1813 and Clark's premises in Wigmore Street London became Clark & Debenham. The young Debenham had wide experience in the textile trade having been apprenticed for some years to a wholesale Nottingham hosiery manufacturer. His and Clark's expertise ensured profits and successes and their trade flourished. London, the centre of social activity, a fashionable playground, was expanding in population. Shopkeepers gravitated towards the West End and thrived on 'society' cravings for new fashions.

By 1905 Debenhams not only acquired a number of old-fashioned businesses but their retail and wholesale trading grew rapidly. The export side developed and premises were established overseas in numerous countries and flourished until the end of the Great War. From 1919 amalgamations and mergers with other 'brand' names such as Marshall & Snelgrove and Harvey Nichols increased Debenhams' strength.

Debenhams ran benevolent societies for staff welfare. It pioneered a dental health service and encouraged its staff to take further education with the help of the Shop Assistant's Union. Female employees benefited and were sent to working women's colleges. There was a Debenhams' Workers Approved Society that protected sick employees. There were also many other 'staff provisions' which benefited the employees. (Those wishing to probe more deeply into the Debenhams' story will find 'Fine Silks & Oak Counters' by Maurice Corina a useful source. It is not a definitive history on Debenhams but rather a "study in shopping from 1778 to 1978").

Behind the City scenes in December 1925 the Drapery Trust (Drapery & General Investment Trust) was being created and negotiations were under way to purchase eight businesses which included Kennards. The transaction was completed in 1926. Debenhams waited in the wings, feeling the effects of the economic difficulties of the period, but came into the limelight the following year, for they bought no less than 75% of the Drapery Trust shares and eventually acquired 99.8%. The fusion of the Drapery Trust with Debenhams made headline news and was called "the creation of the greatest drapery distribution organisation in this country and probably the world". In 1928 Debenhams was listed on the London Stock Exchange, where it traded as an independent company.

The late 1930s and early 1940s had a profound effect on department stores. The ill winds of the Second World War blew havoc on businesses and shortages and bomb damage ruined many a shop and store. Britain's war weary population tired of 'making do and mend' witnessed 'Americana' life styles through the latest cinema film showings of the late 1940s and early 1950s. Britain became a consumer hungry nation which British retailers were to satisfy with the latest merchandise, self-service, self-selecting and brighter shops. A new shopping revolution was on its way into Britain, but many of its war shattered and out of date stores failed to catch the tide of change.

Around the 1950s the number of independent stores was on the decline with rising costs being another reason for the 'family' stores demise. They failed to keep pace with the fast changing world of the speciality shops, multiples, discount and chain stores and were labour intensive and entrenched in the past. Sitting on prime freehold sites in big cities and towns, with death duties that hit these family department stores particularly hard, they became obvious targets, so amalgamations and take-overs were inevitable. Debenhams took over a succession of businesses throughout its time, allowing them to retain their identities and family management in return for capital and a few seats on their board. They realised the importance of long standing family names and traditions, which customers valued. Few shoppers knew of their ownership by or association with Debenhams.

By 1967 the Debenhams' organisation was still expanding. It had grown from a little shop with a 20ft.frontage in Wigmore Street to the largest department store group in the country. (By 1985 the Chairman of The Burton Group successfully bid for 65 of Debenhams' stores and they became

The "old order changeth". Debenhams, which also operates over the top of the Drummond Centre, completed its store in two stages, 1983.

part of the Burton Group plc. although still trading under the name of Debenhams excluding Brown's of Chester).

In 1973 the time had come for Debenhams to impose its corporate identity on virtually all its operations and notice boards appeared in Kennards windows to reveal it was now "A DEBENHAM STORE". On the 16th March 1973 there was a "jointed funeral and christening". Kennards, Croydon's oldest store, was laid to rest after 120 years of trading and renamed Debenhams. The change of name made it "easier for advertising purposes and to identify with the Debenhams group".

It was in the early 1980s when Kennards, Croydon's 'dowager', once dignified and gracious in appearance, drew sentiment and sad countenance from customers on its demise and subsequent

Debenhams' "new look store", c. early 1980s.

Debenhams using every inch of space, c. early 1980s.

Debenhams' menswear, c. early 1980s.

demolition. The store had become dusty and musty in looks and spirit; it became a store ill equipped to carry on and was laid to rest. Kennards was literally lowered into its coffin.

Debenhams made its debut in the form of an American designed store on the same site and its 'coming out' period lasted nearly five years and construction, in two stages, was costly. (The three major store groups, House of Fraser, John Lewis Partnership and Debenhams, spent around £150 million between 1981 and 1984 on such face lifts).

In January 1998 Debenhams demerged from The Burton Group (now known as Arcadia Group plc) and were operating from 87 department stores in the U.K. principally situated in prime high street locations and out of town retail parks. A store operates in Ireland and another overseas in Bahrain, operating under franchise from Debenhams. In February 1999 The Crown Prince of Dubai officially opened Debenhams' latest international franchise store in Dubai, United Arab Emirates

and is the company's third international store to be opened in the Gulf in conjunction with franchise partners, the Alshaya Group.

In March 1999 Debenhams received the highest accolade at the Retail Week Awards when they were voted 'Retailer of the Year 1999'. The award is given to the retailer who "demonstrates outstanding financial performance and drive for innovation and new ideas right across the business". This incorporates merchandising, distribution, marketing, people management and training initiatives. Debenhams announced in the national newspapers in October 1999 that plans to revamp 70 stores at a cost of £120 million is to take place over the next four years. They also plan to build 13 new or relocated stores and recently completed an overhaul of its flagship London store in Oxford Street.

Today Debenhams is one of the leading department store groups and "Britain's favourite department store".

Above: Debenhams North End Croydon in the year 2000.
Below: The Drummond Centre in pedestrianized North End, 2000.

EPILOGUE

Whilst in conversation regarding my 'Surrey Street, Croydon' publication, a Croydonian remarked to me that the sweets sold on a stall in Surrey Street market in yesteryear tasted delicious and said "They don't make them like that anymore". My reply was that we can in fact buy the 'real thing' the home made food and sweet products. But the elderly lady remarked "No, the sugar tastes different and the butter doesn't taste like it once did; no, the ingredients are not the same."

No matter how much we try to emulate, nothing can ever be exactly the same. Kennards has been and gone and has its own place in history but it has left an indelible mark, not just in that span of its life time, but also in people's minds and hearts today. The 'characters' of Kennards were the 'ingredients' of the store, such ingredients as 'Mr.William' Kennard, the founder's son, who was of a kindly disposition and gave constant encouragement and support to his staff. The drive and energies of the managing director Jimmy Driscoll, who dreamt up one exploit after another, the optimist who drove the employees ever forward and boosted their self-esteem. The devoted staff, too numerous to mention, who worked in their loyal manner for their employer. Ingredients that blended well together and made an extraordinary store, which was enhanced with decorative toppings such as the visiting stars who sparkled in their day and the spectacular Christmas festivities along with all the trimmings which kept the customers and their children in constant delight. Although Kennards expanded and developed into a mammoth store, it never lost its family roots. Many an ex-employee regarded Kennards as their family, with such comments as "we loved working there" and "we were like one big happy family".

Although I cannot replicate Kennards' history I hope I have managed to capture not only some of the characters but also a sense of time and atmosphere and even its sense of purpose.

Forget-me-not

ABOUT THE AUTHOR

Vivien Lovett is married with twin sons and lives in West Purley, Surrey. She enjoys giving talks to groups and societies about Surrey Street market, Croydon and has introduced further talks on medieval markets and shops and Kennards department store. She is a committee member on several groups involved in local issues and conservation amongst her other commitments.

Her hobbies include playing the violin and piano, enjoying long walks with her dog Lizzie and gardening. Vivien is currently working on her next Croydon local history publication with another planned for Wallington.

Previous publication: 'Surrey Street, Croydon – A Stall Story'
Published by Frosted Earth

APPENDIX

1824	William Kennard born in Deal, Kent
1853	William Kennard established at 'Warwick House' 7-8 North End Croydon
1853	8.600 customers served
1853	Staff numbered two
1853	Hand Cart deliveries
1859	William Kennard's son – Arthur Grover born ('Mr. Arthur')
1865	William Kennard's son – William Thomas born ('Mr. William')
1865	William Kennard resided at 1 Cavendish Villas, Wellesley Road, Croydon
1880	Main staircase erected (first of three)
1881	Staff numbered 7
1886	North End street renumbering (7 & 8 become 15 & 17)
1887	William Kennard (Founder) died
1892	Kennards also occupied a shop opposite 16 North End 'Manchester House'
1896	Kennards occupied 11 to 17 inclusive
1896	Kennards vacated 'Manchester House'
1901	Eleven horse drawn vehicles
1901	Staff numbered 43
1901	104.587 customers served
1905	Main staircase erected (second of three)
1907	Kennards occupied 11 to 23 inclusive
1911	Kennards occupied 11 to 31 inclusive
1912	Toy Bazaar opened
1920	New (North End) Main Entrance
1920	Small Block added to rear
1921	Staff numbered 250
1921	Hardware Section opened
1922	Main (final) staircase erected
1922	Kennards become a 3 floor establishment
1923	Another 3 floors added to the rear block
1924	Hairdressing Dept & Beauty Parlours opened
1926	Kennards purchased by The Drapery Trust
1927	Debenhams purchased the Drapery Trust
1928	4th floor building opened
1929	Batchelars acquired by Kennards
1929	Sports department opened
1931	Wimbledon store purchased
1931	Main restaurant and Blue Room opened
1932	Cash & Carry Store opened (new block facing Frith Road)
1932	Hedges Yard demolished
1933	Kennards' Gazette
1933	Organ installed in main restaurant
1933	Staff numbered 875
1934	Cold storage room built
1934	Staff restaurant – new building
1935	Kennards' library opened
1935	New roof completed (Keeley Road extension)
1936	New roof top restaurant opened
1936	Extension to Keeley Road
1936	'Mr. Arthur' Arthur Grover Kennard died
1936	Staff numbered 1.000
1937	New car park
1937	A 300 seating Colour Cinema theatre opened
1937	Staff numbered 1.200
1937	8 million customers served
1937	Perfumery Department opened
1937	Series of Shops opened (main arcade)
1937	New Snack Bar
1937	Rejuvenation of Cash & Carry Store
1938	North End arcade front (grand new frontage)
1939	New canopied North End Store front built (weather protection)
1940	Staff numbered 1.100
1940	New Wing added adjoining Keeley Road entrance (now 10½ acre site)
1944	'Mr. William' William Thomas Kennard died
1946	Redhill store purchased
1947	Estate Agency opened
1951	Staff numbered 1.027
1951	6.381.933 customers served
1951	Modern motor fleet including articulated vehicles
1956	Wimbledon store sold
1959	Ground floor redesigned
1959	Supermarket
1960	Extensive modernisation carried out
1960	Staff numbered 1.000
1961	Self Service Restaurant opened 'The Luncheonette'
1963	Debenhams sold Kennards of Redhill
1965	New Fashion floor on 1st floor, involving 17 departments
1967	New ladies hairdressing salon, modernised and refitted
1967	Car accessory shop on lower ground floor
1968	New Food Hall
1968	New Crown Hill entrance
1968	New 'Man's shop' at Main front entrance, ground floor
1973	Kennards name officially changed to Debenhams
1979	Hedgis Yard (main arcade) closed
Early 1980s	Kennards demolished

ACKNOWLEDGEMENTS

I would dearly like to thank the numerous people who sent me their stories, photographs, detailed maps and information for this publication, for without them valuable material would undoubtedly have been lost forever.

My very special thanks to all of the following people for without their help the Kennards' story would have been difficult to tell. My dearest husband Leslie Whitehouse, who said he would not 'survive' another book (after my 'Surrey Street, Croydon' publication), but realised I would not survive if I did not continue writing! My son Andrew for relieving me on the 'home front' so that I could concentrate on Kennards. Geoff Morris who closely followed my Kennards' time trail and gave me valuable information and photographs. Robin Kennard for his valued assistance and for writing the Foreword to the book and supplying many photographs and archive material on his great grandfather's store. Bernard Harding gave me valuable information and the loan of photographs for the 'sister stores' chapter. Both he and his father had been in managerial positions in Kennards. The National Motor Museum at Beaulieu for information and identifying several vehicles used or exhibited at Kennards. Chris & Dennis Greenwood for their hospitality and useful knowledge on 'mannequins'. My cousin Miriam Baharier (nee Garcia), for the loan of archive material on the Croydon Times Bunny Club. Alan Schpot, Store Manager of Debenhams in Croydon for the kind loan of rare photographic material and for his valued assistance. Mike Coffey of the Cottage Homes for informative material. Valuable archive material was obtained from Croydon Local Studies Library and Archives Service with the friendly assistance from Steve Roud and his team. Special thanks to The Bourne Society for valued advice and support. My appreciation to Croydon Museum & Heritage who assisted with sponsored and thanks to Adrienne Bloch the Heritage Development Officer and her team for their support and advice.

I cannot thank Derek Bradford enough for his input. He edited my typescript and reproduced not only the majority of the photographs for my Surrey Street publication, but also played an important role in reproducing and enlarging virtually all of the Kennards' photographs. His expertise in editing and checking my manuscript on numerous occasions was an extremely time consuming task. Without his help and encouragement I would not have had the courage to write about this mammoth store. My very grateful thanks and appreciation to Debenhams (Head Office) Welbeck Street, London, especially to Ceinwen Morris, the Debenhams Group Customer Relations Manager who gave her support and time in locating the 'Kennards' collection'. Access to several 'scrap books' of newspaper archive material and the many visits by my husband and myself to photograph from the original archive albums in her offices was crucial to the story telling of Kennards. Without Debenhams' support and Ceinwen Morris's assistance I would not have much of the wonderful photographic material for this book.

I do apologise most sincerely if I have omitted any person or persons. This is quite unintentional. I also apologise for omitting many stories because of lack of space.

BIBLIOGRAPHY

Cabinet Maker 1937
Coaching Journal & Bus Review 1970 published by Travel & Transport Ltd
Corsetry & Underwear Journal 1937 published by Circle Publications Ltd
Croydon Airport 'The Australian Connection' by Douglas Cluett
Croydon Airport 1928–1939 by Douglas Cluett, Joanna Nash, Bob Learmonth
Croydon Focus published by The Croydon Society
Croydon at Work published by The Croydon Society & Croydon Chamber of Commerce & Industry
Croydon in the 1940s/1950s published by the Croydon Natural History & Scientific Society
Croydon, the Story of a Hundred Years published by the Croydon Natural History & Scientific Society
Fine Silks & Oak Counters – Debenhams 1778-1978 – by Maurice Corina
Furnishing Record 1937
Furniture World 1935
Kennards' Gazettes 1933–1939
Life in Wartime Britain by E.R. Chamberlin
Pictorial Record, Croydon 1913
Royal Russell School – A History – by S. Hopewell
Shopping in Croydon Guide late 1920s
Shops by Renee Huggett
Shops & Shopping 1800–1914 by Alison Adburgham
The Children's Outfitter 1937
The Drapers Organiser 1937
The Drapers Record 1937
The Outfitter 1937
The Store 1937
Women's Wear News 1938

NEWSPAPERS
Coulsdon & Purley Times 1937
Croydon Advertiser
Croydon Times
Surrey County Mail 1938
Sutton Times & Cheam Mail 1938
The Purley Review 1929
The Times & County Mail 1962
Town & County News 1929
Wallington & Carshalton Times 1937

CELEBRITY CALLS

The following list of Kennards celebrity stars is by no means complete, but is taken from archive material obtained to date. Below are listed the personalities who were more well known or played a 'role' in the store.

1920s
Miss Gladys Cooper (Beauty Demonstration)
Miss Fay Compton (New 4th Floor Extension)

1930s
Madeleine Carrol (Judges Croydon's Beauty Queen)
Phylis Neilson-Terry
Leonard Henry, Clapham & Dwyer (main restaurant)
Norman Long (Kennards new restaurant)
Blue Bird Racing Car (Exhibition)
Her Grace The Duchess of Athol (Scottish Linen Exhibition)
Mabel Constanduros
The Dagenham Girl Pipers
'Zenobia' Lily of the Valley Cabaret
Two Gun Rix – Wild West Show
Miss Dodo Watts
Hayden Wood (dedicates new restaurant organ)
Billy Booey & his Olympia Clowns
'Young Kendow' England's Strongest Man
Judy Kelly
Dennis Wheatley (New library)
Prince Paul Troubetskoy (Beauty Parlour)
Miss Gladys Wood (Lancashire Cotton Week)
Miss Enid Stamp-Taylor (Batchelars showhouse)
Lupino Lane & Teddy St. Denis (Baby Competition)
The Hal Swain Band (Restaurant entertainment)
To-Ya the Ice Family
Mr. Castang the Ape Man
Hassan's Real Arab Snake Charmers
Hassan & his Indian Troupe
John Lester's Midget Circus
Miss Helen Vinson (82nd Birthday celebrations)
Kiano's Hilo Hawaiians (82nd Birthday celebrations)
Jean Kram the Parisian Juggler (Kennards café)
Miss Susan Gray (Fashion Artist)
Six Anglo American Beauties (Fashion Parades)
Prunella Stack
The Great Omi (The Tattooed Wonder)
Rex Kayanagh the 'Daredevil' film car driver
Miss Nina Mae McKinney (Buyers Gift Week Cup)
Leon Volpre's Indoor Circus
Elwyn Smith (The lightning artist)
Prince Zuluamkah
Band of the Cameron Highlanders

Cardi the Conjurer
Mr. Jackson the Manipulative Specialist
Ali Baba & his Troupe of Indian performers
Miss Ivy Russell (World's Strongest Girl)
Zane Baynes (Singer in Restaurant)
Maurice Sinnett (Singer in Restaurant)
Jean Batten (Buyers Gift Week Cup)
Dr. Ford and his Chinese Flea Circus
Chief Blue Sky & His Braves (Wild West Show)
Dr. N'Gai The Mystery Man
Madame Monty (Clairvoyant & Advice Specialist)
Madam Bassie (Horoscope & Psychological Reading)
Musa the Indian Palmist
Mlle Veronica (Heala Ray Health Centre/Ballito stand)
Marie Victoria & Marquita (Spanish dancers in Restaurant)
Eric Filby (Surrey Table Tennis)
Miss Edna Wood (Buyer's Cup)
Howard Spring (New Library)
Claude Dampier & Billie Carlisle (Golfing Film)
Albert Ray (Darts demonstration)
Chili Bouchier (84th Birthday Celebrations)
The Filmland Glamour Girls (Fashion Parades)
Sam Melville the Singing Trumpeter from South Africa
Lenardo the Singing Accordionist
Snow White & the Seven Dwarfs
12 Queens of Loveliness (from Women's Fair, Olympia)
Barbara Blair
June Duprez
Prince Zulamkah & His Native Africans
Ju Ju & His Native Band
'Kushorney' the Mystery Mind (Restaurant & Parade Floor)

1940s
Jack Warner (Blue Pencil Week)
Godfrey Winn
Ernie Lotinga
Lady Goodenough & Admiral Sir Wm. Goodnough
Duke of Norfolk (South of England Red Cross Rabbit Show)
Charles Coburn
Owen Nairs (Fuel Exhibition)
Commander Campbell
Lord Croft (Under Secretary State for War)
Elsie & Doris Waters (Battle for Fuel Exhibition)
Daphne Kelf (Singing Mannequin)
The Band of the East Yorkshire Regiment (Prisoner of War Fund)
Zona the famous Saxo-Xylophoniste (Restaurant Entertainment)
Prince Zulamkah (Holidays at Home Entertainment)

Professor Niblo & his Bird
Sandy Powell & his Ventriloquist doll Danny
Snr. Lt. Timokin (Red Army)
Ronnie Waldeman (B.B.C)
Richard Murdoch
Group Captain Jimmie Rankin
Group Captain 'Tin Legs' Bader
Group Captain 'Sailor' Malan
Group Captain 'Cats' Eyes' Cunningham
Wing Commander Drake
Michael Rennie
Joe Baksi
Bert Couzens
Sheila Sim
Margaret Lockwood
Jean Kent
Linden Travers
Avril Angers
Sid Fields
Albert Whelan
Stars of 'Ice Cycles'
Five Smith Brothers

1950s
Guy Middleton
Dirk Bogarde
Lana Morris
Jimmy Hanley
Sir Harold Scott (K.C.B.Commissioner of Police)
Petula Clark
Christine Norden
Jeremy Spenser
Maj. Gen. Leon Johnson (United States Airforce)
Maj. Gen. Sir Ernest Cowell. (K.B.E)
Air Commodore McEvoy
Googie Withers

OTHER VISITORS
Duke of Gloucester
Prince Monolulu
Lord Leverhulme
Edith Day
Anna May Wong
Marie Burke
Commander King Hall (M.P.)
Mr. Willink (Minister of Health 1946–7)

Numerous Mayors of Croydon
Numerous Members of Parliament
Dr. Fisher. Archbishop of Canterbury
John Stuart
Muriel Angelus
Jack Smith the Miners M.P.
Harry Welchman
Emanual Shinwell the Minister of Fuel
Will Fyffe
Fred Davis (Billiards Champion)
Sidney Lee (Amateur Billiards Champion)
Flotsam and Jetsam
Owen Nares
Freddie Grisewood
Billie Cotton and His Band
Felix Mendelsohn and his Band
Harold Ramsey
Archibald Joyce
Margaret Bannerman
Norman Long
Judy Kelly
Jane Carr
Miss Margaret Bondfield
Tommy Trinder
Nat D Ayer
Arthur Tracey (The Street Singer)
Helen McKay (Artist)
Sir George Thomas
Walter Lindrum
Admiral Sir William James (KCB. M.P.)
Lady Duff Gordon (the famous 'Lucille') dress designer
Prunella Stack (later Lady David Douglas Hamilton)
Gladys Cooper
Lady Fletcher
Wanda Rotha
Jonah Barrington
Roy Hay (BBC Garden expert)
Sir Neville Wilkinson
Jimmie Wilde
Jack Bloomfield
Jane Welsh
Barbara Blair
Jane Cain
Humble (Cyclist)
Giovanni
Pat Phoenix

PHOTOGRAPH CREDITS

I would like to sincerely thank the following for their most valued photographic contribution towards Kennards. Every effort has been made to obtain the original source of photographic material in this publication. In some cases photographs were secured in archive albums so credit has been given to the 'holder'.

ROBIN KENNARD for (Chapter 1).William Kennard & double fronted shop. (Chapter 2) 'Mr & Mrs. William'. Glass Cases. Kennards vans. Builders on scaffolding. Two builders. North End street scene. Main Entrance. (Chapter 3). Mr. Driscoll portrait (Chapter 4). Bentwood chairs (Chapter 6). Toy Bazaar. Prints. Modern Merchandising. Arts & Needlework. Bags and trunks. Glass & China. Linen. Foreign Fancy 1912 & 1923. Cash desks. Counting house. Grand opening. Beads & Stationery. Haberdashery. Tudor café. Fancy section. Bedding. Furnishing. Sports coats. Staircase. Fire engine. Main showroom. Cotton prints. (Chapter 7). The Kennardians & Management. (Chapter 11). Clock Days. (Chapter 13) Easter Eggs. Bunkumsnorus.

DEBENHAMS (WELBECK STREET LONDON) for (Chapter 2) North End (arcade) walkway. Showcases. Kennards vans. Shop front.(Chapter 3). Batchelars showcase & 'show' room. (Chapter 4). Hedgis Yard. Frith Road entrance. New store entrance. (Chapter 6). Interior dept. Library. Hats. Cash & Carry Frith Isle. Bunn Shop. Thrift Bank. Dogs Toggery. Kennels. Restaurant. Quick Service Counter. Cheetahs in restaurant. Shop floor. Mlle. Veronica. (Chapter 8) Grand staircase. (Chapter 11). White elephant sale. Sales girls. Mr. Driscoll in car. Duster sale. Sainsbury's stock purchase. Kennards delivery vans. Crystal Palace interior. Kennards bike stand. Buyer's gift week. (Chapter 12). Fay Compton. African village. Indian village. Golf course. Claude Dampier. Girls with buckets. (Chapter 13). Railway rides. Roof top. Cock-a-doodle-do Farm. Childrens' roundabout. (Chapter 14). Father Christmas on tractor. Father Christmas in North End. Wild West street scene. Chief Blue Sky & His Braves. (Chapter 15). Rubber salvage. Punch & Judy. Pets Department. Air raid shelter. (Chapter 16). Pet shop.

DEBENHAMS OF CROYDON for (Chapter 2) 1893 North End 'Kennard Bros'. Buckworth North End. (Chapter 3). Dempsters reference (Chapter 4). Batchelars store (Chapter 6). Supermarket. Beauty Parlour 1940 (Chapter 11). Kennards factory sale. (Chapter 12). 'Bluebird'. (Chapter 13). Drummond Road caged animals. (Chapter 15) Letter.(Chapter 17). Model on escalator. Male model. Debenhams shelves. Two stage development Debenhams store.

CROYDON STUDIES LIBRARY 1895 Ordinance Survey map. (Chapter 6) Clothes fashions. (Chapter 14) Xmas North End

THE CROYDON ADVERTISER GROUP for those photographs individually credited.

In addition I would like to thank the following. J. MARSHALL (Chapter 1) The Founder. G. HANA PHOGRAPHERS (Chapter 2) Kennards North End. North End Frontage 1923. (Chapter 6) Perfumery Dept. (Chapter 12). Kennards North End 'Tea Dances'.

CHORLEY HANDFORD (Chapter 2) 2 arcade window cases (Chapter 6) Internal dept/Mr. Harding, La Belle Eve. Car Park. Cash girls. Dressing Rooms. Mannequin parade. Wolsely window. Wolsely Mannequin. Kennards and Batchelars frontage 1951 (Chapter 11). Kennards fashion show. Fashion parade. (Chapter 12). Jean Batten. (Chapter 13). Cheetahs. (Chapter 10). Kennards. Redhill new frontage. (Chapter 14). Hospital visit. (Chapter 15). Incendiary bombs. Air bomb attack. (Chapter 16) Travel Exhibition.

CORSETS SILHOUETTE LTD. (Chapter 8) corset advert. MRS. MARTIN (Chapter 8) Chef. Staff outing. COTTAGE HOMES MILL HILL. (Chapter 8) Cottage ceremony. BERNARD HARDING (Chapter 10) Kennards of Wimbledon, corner and side view. Hove store. (Chapter 11). Crystal palace fashion (Chapter 13). Fancy Dress. PHELPS & MARCHANT (Chapter 10) two photos of the Redhill store queue. HAMN'S PHOTO-NEWS SERVICE LTD. (Chapter 10) Kennards van. C.B.HARRISON (Chapter 12) Bukta Swim Suits. MRS. HILBOURNE (Chapter 14) 1940 Xmas. MIRIAM BAHARIER (Chapter 14) Cowboy Uncle Jack. PLANET NEWS LTD.(Chapter 12) Baby competition. J.W.GRAVES of DAGENHAM (Chapter 13) Dagenham Drummer. SALISBURY PHOTO PRESS (Chapter 13) Dutch girls. E.A.SWEETMAN & SON LTD. (Chapter 8) Russell School postcard. SURREY MIRROR (Chapter 15) Gert & Daisy. JOHN GENT COLLECTION (Chapter 14) Father Christmas. F.W.BERRY (Chapter 15) Fire squad on roof. GEOFF MORRIS (Chapter 14) Advert on Bridge. WIDE WORLD PHOTOS (Chapter 15) painted stockings. FOX STUDIOS PHOTOS (Chapter 15) stocking/male assistant. Growers market. Silk stocking sale. MRS. ROSA WOODS (chapter 16) Tudor shop. Mr.Woods & shop. DAVID COX (Chapter 16) shoe repairs. WINDSOR SPICE LTD. (Chapter 10) New Show dept. MRS. ANDERSON (Chapter 6) Restaurant. HAYCOCK PRESS, London (Chapter 12) Fancy dress. MAX and MORITZ (Chapter 12) J.P. Bamber, Blackpool.